Paris Aston

David Aston

Polar Stroke

David Aston

Foreword

I first met David one Friday when he stopped by my office at Chest Heart & Stroke Scotland for a chat. David was volunteering for us in the Finance Department following his stroke, though it was clear he found getting to Edinburgh from the Borders exhausting, and he needed a sit down and a chat before getting down to his volunteering tasks. But David is a determined man, as you will discover on reading his book. This is a remarkable story of perseverance, an amazing account of teamwork (and an understanding of how weaknesses as well as strengths can be melded into a successful team) and some glorious one-liners which had me laughing out loud.

Stroke turns life upside-down and inside-out – for family and friends as well. It strikes out of the blue, and life is never the same again. It's also one of the least recognised causes of death and disability, trailing well behind cancer, dementia and heart conditions in the nation's consciousness, yet just as cruel. David's volunteering pattern has moved on, and he now helps by speaking about his experiences at events. I miss our Friday chats, but am honoured and delighted to be involved in a small way in his book.

Penelope Blackwell, Director of Fundraising, Chest Heart & Stroke Scotland

Acknowledgements

The schedule of acknowledgements is more reflective of my current life then it is of just writing the book and so obviously the first name published here has to be Jacki Aston. Jacki is my wife and has shown incredible patience in her dealings with me after the crash. I am not the same person as I was and it is with incredible luck that Jacki has stood by me.

Since I had the crash, there has been one charity which, before the crash, I didn't know existed but, afterwards, they were fantastic to me, particularly the service organiser who ran the local service for stroke victims in Peebles. Whilst running the club, she introduced me to a young woman whom would not acknowledge the reason for thanking her, but she is the first person I've met who was younger than me when she had the stroke and has effectively dealt with it. Also worth thanking from the charity are Penelope Blackwell who wrote my foreword, Jackie Erskine and John Cuthbertson.

I thank Anna Nicholson for helping with the cover; Richard Harlow who set up my website; Richard Leeson for guiding me on how to publish the book and the Peebles Round Table.

Index

1   Setting a goal

I was in my mid-thirties and had more or less achieved what I wanted to from a work point of view. Of course I had other objectives but I had achieved a certain amount. I knew that from a career point of view, I would have to leave Baker Tilly or at least leave the Basingstoke office as I was the youngest and newest Audit Partner and the fact was, the office was too small to attract the kind of clients Baker Tilly wanted and too expensive for the clients we had pre-merger. These were also the clients that I fared best with as we were able and expected to give much more advice than we were at Baker Tilly.

I say pre-merger because legally two partnerships have to merge. However, the reality was that Baker Tilly had a couple of hundred partners and I joined from Harris Walters which had a total of seven and not all of them joined. I totally agreed with the logic behind both parties with the decision to merge but unfortunately it had not gone to plan and now I had a decision to make. I had got to the point where I realised that, although it was a very nice and very well paid job, I could go no further with the job as it stood and I, therefore, had to leave or accept the situation. I thought about this for a long time but gradually came around to the fact I should stay and seek my personal objectives outside of this. With hindsight I made the wrong decision as, a few years later, I had to leave the firm because it was going in a different direction from where I wanted to go. However, it gave me the opportunity to achieve what I thought was impossible.

Having decided, at that point, to stay at Baker Tilly I decided to set myself a goal and then to set about achieving it. I had no idea about the goal in terms of what I should do or about how to find out about it, but as I had learned, if you have an idea it is amazing where it will take you.

I had just been to China on a charitable walk across the Great Wall of China. The event had been set up with Whizz Kidz but it was through the Round Table, an organisation I had been a member of for years and as far as travelling goes, I have always had good experiences. The trip itself was fantastic and the memories I have from China are great but when I think about the walk it wasn't difficult or challenging at all and I am afraid I overestimated the walking part of the trip.

I say overestimated the challenge that lay in store but that was probably deliberate. They wanted everyone to finish the walk, collect them their money, and leave happy. To be fair, they achieved that and the Round Table members made it a trip I thoroughly enjoyed, but the lack of an expected challenge bugged me. I decided my goal should be travel-based. Travel was something I loved and wanted to do more of. I was now established at work and, for the first time in my life, I could do more.

Whilst working for Harris Walters before the merger into Baker Tilly I helped a man, whom I had known professionally for some time, when his flat burnt down and he needed a home quickly. As I had lots of space, he moved in for a short time. He is probably the most extensive traveller I have met. He has been almost anywhere and has some fantastic stories to tell, often they involve him being badly treated but he had recovered and just deals with it. I was becoming an interested traveller but, after having conversations with this man, I was convinced I should do more.

I had missed the point of the Chinese walk and thought I needed to become a lot fitter, as did the two Winchester Round Table members who were also going on the trip, but alas the trip was a money-making exercise and was actually quite easy for me. I joined the Winchester lads who were going on the trip for some practice walks around Winchester before we went to China. I had started seeing a girl around this time and she came on one walk with us. I had always suspected she was fitter than we were but I hadn't realised how much fitter until this walk. The Chinese holiday turned out to be incredible. The first week organised by Whizz Kidz was a walk along the Great Wall which, although disappointing from a fitness viewpoint, it was brilliant being a Tabler on a Round Table trip. By coincidence, the Tabler who I was booked to share a tent with, whom I had never met before had also booked a week's holiday afterwards and he seemed good fun so we agreed to spend the week in China together. This week was, without doubt, my favourite holiday time up until then, probably because it was so different to the UK. I also ranked Kenya but we were staying with a UK holiday company and they kept it fairly British and we just went on a transfer to different nature reserves so, although fantastic, it did not have the impact of China. Remembering both these trips convinced me I should travel somewhere interesting and do it in a challenging way. The idea posed and the questions started but were based on where, when and how.

At this time I had gone out with another girl for about three weeks and I hadn't mentioned it, but I had been considering completing the expedition, just didn't know where. I was planning to discuss this with her but she decided to leave me, and to be fair quite rightly, because I was totally self-centred at that point. Interestingly, the way she left me was startling and, in itself, very motivating! She said she was going as she was a lot more sporting than me. She was of course, but it was irritating she picked that as an excuse. However, it made me more determined than ever that it would be a physical challenge going somewhere unusual. Still I had to work out where, when and how.

I had considered doing an around-the-world yacht race but I could not afford a year out or even consider the training involved. I did think about just doing one leg but decided that actually I would just be annoyed by that by leaving the team to continue the race.

I also thought of a mountain climbing expedition but, to make it memorable, I would have to do a lot of training and work up to it. It may sound stupid, but I didn't fancy that. Doing something like going to the base camp of Mount Everest would annoy me, as there would be people going higher. I could think of nothing and then I was sent on a leadership course from the office.

The course was run by a group of people who had done an around-the-world yacht race but also appeared in a race to the magnetic north pole. I don't know what the course taught about leadership but it settled the matter, I was going to the magnetic north pole, only from now on in it was known as the North Pole.

The first thing to do was to get in contact with the organiser, Jock. This proved a bit more fortuitous than I thought as the people who ran the course hated Jock and were organising their own trip, but fortunately they still had Jock's details written down. The course organisers were extremely good travellers being army officers and they wished to make the North Pole trip as hard as it could be whereas Jock wanted accessibility for all, and I needed it to be made as simple as possible.

2   Preparation

I had a brief chat to Jock on the phone and I explained I was totally new to this and, I meant totally new. I thought this would upset him but he explained, providing I took the training seriously, I would be able to make it and he agreed to send me some literature about the trip but warned me I should get it back to him quickly as he was going to be recruiting for the next trip shortly. I completed the literature as well as possible but I could say nothing about previous trips and although I mentioned China as my best previous trip it really meant nothing.

I had expected this would be sufficient for Jock to remove me from his list but, to my eternal gratitude, he persevered. His view was if you want to, providing you train properly, you can. As a result I had agreed to go on a recruitment drive in December 2003 to go to the North Pole in April and May of 2005.

I thought I ought to warn my parents about my trip and I thought it was best to mention this before I actually got recruited as I didn't expect to be recruited and, on discussion with my parents, neither did they. Clearly this was a surprise to my parents that if I got recruited, I was going and they did accept that, even though they were not impressed. The other person I had to warn was the Office Managing Partner but I thought I'd wait until I knew whether I was going to be accepted on the trip.

The recruitment day arrived and I wasn't sure where I was going. I was nervous about the day as a whole, so I left in ample time in case anything went wrong. It didn't and I arrived with hours to spare. The day itself was very interesting. Half the people had other team members whilst the other half were without a team and they would ultimately have to get a team. This meant I was chatting up the non-teamed people but I still had to work hard to get recruited.

The recruitment day was split into work sessions and an interview. The work sessions were fairly difficult because they were to do with being at the pole and I had not done it before. The only part of the sessions I remember was having a list of items we had to place in order of how we would keep them. It was quite difficult but I must have done all right. I had been dreading the interview but the first question was "do you know the cost"? I replied "yes" and informed them of the amount I had been told. This made me feel good as I knew they were not worried about whether I had the skill or not, merely whether I could afford it and that I definitely wanted to go. This led to the next question of "how will you pay for it"? I replied "by increasing the mortgage" and they seemed very happy with that. The rest of the questions were technical matters but they kept emphasising that if I wanted to go they would make sure I could go. I said goodbye to them but I knew they would become like my family for the next two years.

I mentioned this to a friend that I was going, expecting he wouldn't believe me and he would just leave it alone, but he had the opposite approach. We went out for the night on Friday and I was amazed how many people in Winchester already knew about the trip and wanted to talk about it. It was probably just as well as it gave me the motivation to get going. I would let Christmas happen but then I would ask work for all my holiday in one hit and just begin the training.

Christmas 2003 became frustrating as all I was interested in was going to the North Pole. My family knew I was going and whilst my mother was terrified, the rest of the family thought it was fantastic. My nephews and niece were all young but they were old enough to understand it was a one-off trip which very few people had achieved.

Back at work I decided I needed to get permission from the Office Managing Partner as I would take all my holiday. I had not really considered him rejecting my application but I think I would still have gone; only I would need another job afterwards. It is a funny thing about telling people about the North Pole, the majority of people get it immediately but about a quarter don't get it originally and a few will never get it.

One Partner I asked was of the middle camp. He didn't really get it to start with but he was very enthusiastic by the end. He did say he would ask the Regional Partner. I said there would be a lot of marketing to be done and of course I was happy for Baker Tilly to be named as helping me go. I didn't know how to take his response but I shouldn't have worried. He mentioned this to the Regional Partner and he got it immediately. I don't know what happened at the meeting but I received a phone call from him and from the firm's Chief Partner.

They were ecstatic with the idea and were even talking about paying for some of the trip, which I was very pleased and, equally very surprised, with. The Senior Partner was very keen about the North Pole and he actually worried me a bit with how much he knew about the trip. This made me determined I had to go now. The Office Managing Partner had got the role now and was equally as enthusiastic but he was from a positon of little knowledge and he was looking forward to getting the information almost as much as me. I had said I was prepared to do marketing for this and it wasn't long before they got involved. Most of this would be done from our office but the national team also wanted to get involved. They had an idea of me getting a monthly a blog on our website of how the training was going. I hated this idea, but once I had finished each month, I had a written article of how it was going which, with hindsight, was fantastic.

Doing the blog was hard work because nothing really changed over time. There were certain fitness levels which I had to overcome and I was able to refer to them each month and organised events for training were also included, but finding the link to it all was very difficult. Having said that, once I had finished it, it gave me a written record of how well the training was going.

I spoke to a marketing girl one day and she said that the blog is actively being followed by several people and if Baker Tilly was entered into Google, I actually come up first. I probably should have checked this but it didn't matter if it was top or not as what was important was that people were genuinely interested in the fact that an eight stone weakling who ordinarily worked as an Accountant was going to the North Pole.

Just before I signed up for the trip one of my friends was going to move to Australia and he was currently living with me as he had gone to an estate agent about letting his flat out and it suddenly got let. Quite rightly, he didn't want to waste having his flat let so I agreed for him to stay with me. Part of this relationship was that I would fly to Perth in Australia to see him, and, never one to miss out on a holiday I was now going.

The week before I went, he emailed me with some bad news. He said it was fine for me to go but he was going on a diving course and it was the same time as I was going to be there. He did have friends and family over there but he would not be there apart from very briefly at the start and finish. This was unfortunate, but not a disaster. I would still stay in his house but would not really see him. I decided I would travel with a couple of his friends the first week and then continue by myself.

The first week we headed down from his house in Freemantle towards the wine growing region for a few days. This was a great tour and it really made us realise the space in that area we were driving for miles and they considered this a short tour! The wine was fantastic and obviously we underwent a wine-tasting tour, but the best thing about this was going on a dolphin cruise. We went on a quick cruise offshore to look for a school of dolphins and were able to play with the dolphins. Some people had got in and were swimming with the dolphins but they weren't allowed to hence we didn't go swimming.

I then decided to go to Rottnest Island where his half-sister would accommodate me for the night. From a training viewpoint, this was excellent as it is a fairly small island approximately twenty five miles in circumference, which proved a great training exercise. I then went to their holiday home to be fed. Rottnest Island or Rotto as it is known is famous for having Quokka's there, a type of very friendly island marsupial, probably because they eat virtually anything. They had a holiday home there and had invited several friends and family over. Although I originally knew no one they were incredibly friendly and particularly interested in the North Pole so I was easily able to get involved with them. They kept mentioning Bundaberg which is Australian rum but for some reason has a polar bear logo. I still have never managed to taste it, but have always thought if it since.

The second week I was pretty much on my own so I thought I would take a couple of tours and the rest of the time I would spend in Freemantle or cross the river to Perth. Perth surprised me because it is well known worldwide but it is small and, having realised this, I spent more time in Freemantle although I did book a couple of bus tours. These were incredible as firstly I was amazed by the distance we covered in a day and secondly the type of things we saw was totally different from the UK. I think it was the space again. We went to various places but I think the most amazing was Wave Rock which is a huge, and I mean huge, rock that had eroded to leave a perfect wave shape, in the middle of nowhere.

I had completed one month's blog when an office person rang me again, officially about a potential client of mine but we spent far longer talking about the North Pole and he reiterated how good an idea the blog was, so I had to keep going with it. The fact I was going to the North Pole had got out at a high level in the firm but not really at a broad level so it was decided, at least in the Basingstoke office, that everyone needed to know so an e-mail was sent around to everyone telling them. The Partner coordinating this did it very well and, more than just telling them I was going, he actually gave a little break down of the trip and, in particular, the dangers there might be. We were still a month or so before the group training started but as far as the firm was concerned the leadership and the local office were fully aware, so now I had to go.

Before I had even gone on the first group session the marketing team were all over this and they got me involved in a local radio station, a local television program and a local newspaper. The first radio program had decided they would call me for a chat live and on air. Obviously I accepted, but I didn't really know what to expect. I waited in a staff meeting room and the phone rang, I was on air and it had started. They only spoke to me for a couple of minutes and actually, it was quite easy. I knew what I was doing but in fact no one else did so as long as I was sensible no one could question it. One point that did throw me was when he asked about the Soviets getting there with tanks in 1960. Obviously I knew nothing about this but said our trip was different because we were walking so this seemed sufficient.

A few days later I had a couple of people come for a television program and I still just took the same view, they didn't know as long as I said something that was sensible I would be okay and I never saw the program but I understand it was fine. I also had a newspaper interview to do and the day could not have been better for it. I went into work as normal, although I needed to leave at around 3pm to get back in time. As I was driving home it started to snow and snow properly. There was lightning in the air as well; I had never seen this before or since. The newspaper guy came and took a couple of pictures of me and asked a string of standard questions and went, but because of the snow the pictures were extraordinary.

Back at work the next day it transpired that I had left at the right time. Some of the people in the office had left at the normal time and couldn't get out of Basingstoke and had to stay overnight in a hotel. Before the first training session I didn't really know what I could do that would be sensible for the North Pole so I just decided I would get as fit as possible. I used to train for about an hour before work with weights and I thought that would be enough. At that stage it might have been, but I doubted it and I missed a few morning training sessions.

The first training was in March and before this I was pretty aware that putting on weight would be my main problem but on the training course Jock confirmed this in no uncertain terms, telling us that everyone lost at least a stone and usually two, he also stated that we should have a Body Mass Index of a minimum of twenty because we would lose so much weight. This meant I had to weigh just over ten stone, at that given time I was just under nine stone and I had never been able to put on weight. The group training session in March was a delightful introduction to the race as I was able to meet with other people who were interested in the trip and rather than all the marketing hype I was doing at work I was able to talk in detail about the technical aspects of it. I was still not aware of what team I would be in but I now knew which members had a team already and I pretty much knew who I wanted to be with and I had to make them want me. I would not physically be as good as anyone else so I had to choose other techniques. There would be a couple more months before we decided on the other teams.

I hadn't really thought about the teams as such but obviously Jock had as he seemed to allow exactly the right amount of time for this. We had long enough to know which people we liked and also long enough to bond as a team. The format of the first few sessions was that we did something to show what level of fitness we had and then we had some technical training about the trip and coping with appalling weather. This time we did circuit training which was basically impossible. Most of the circuit was physically very hard and there was one thing I just couldn't do. It was a rope aspect and we had to climb the rope from top to bottom without being given any help from the rope, for example knots.

They did show us how we could use the rope to produce a step and doing this three or four times you could climb the rope. I managed to do two a couple of times but never any more so I got about half way on some circuits but I had to accept I couldn't get to the top. The rest of the circuit hurt me badly but I could do it. The circuit training seemed to go on for hours but I think it was literally one hour with a very short break after half an hour. I knew it would be tough but now I knew just how tough getting to the North Pole would be. That was one hour, admittedly most hours of my trip would not be that tough but we had several hours one after the other.

The general training all seemed reasonably alright. The trainers covered the main points we would cover and they continually reemphasised that it was just about common sense and accepting that it was cold and making sure you always had the necessary gear on. At the base camp I once thought I didn't need a cap as I was just popping outside for a few seconds but wow I was wrong. After that I became very good at wearing the right kit.

The March training was over and I was very tired driving back from London to Winchester, but still incredibly excited about the trip. These people went on the trip every two years because they wanted anyone who wanted to get there to have a good chance. The people I had met at the leadership course had decided they would make it an annual event, which was great if you were really good but would have been a disaster for me.

I was still working full time and I had to think about writing the blog. I decided that my blog would have quite a lot about the organised training on it because that was for me an eye-opener, not only as to how much was involved, but also just keeping your head and being sensible no matter what confronted you was probably most of the battle. In addition, all my blogs would have a lot about the weight gain as gaining a bit more than a stone would be easy for most but to me it would be incredibly difficult. Throughout the build-up I would have to put on weight and I wasn't sure how to do this or even if I could. The first thing I had to do was improve my eating, or at least I had to eat more often. I was very good; in fact I still am, at only eating when I was hungry and needed to have food. This meant I had to eat more particularly at work. I took two strategies for this; the first was to go out for lunch as much as possible and the second to start helping myself to food in the kitchen.

Going out for lunch proved easier than I thought. Firstly all the local professionals in and around Basingstoke enjoyed going out with me, they never wanted to discuss work but rather how I was getting on with the trip training. We did get some work out of this because, although we never really discussed work, it was a given we could do it and so, when they needed work doing, they would ring. The main thing was that they would arrange lunch with us. The second reason was that my Tax Partner, a mutual friend, was fully on board and when we didn't have a chance for lunch with other professionals, we would just go together.

This Tax Partner was proving a far better Partner than he would know as, invariably I was having lunch with him or with him and other professionals and, though we tried to spread the conversation equally it was me they wanted to listen to. I didn't realise how much of my trip training he had to listened to until one lunchtime I was giving a fairly in depth answer about burying the tent in snow because snow was easier than using rope and hooks along the side and he piped up 'the thing I find most impressive was you told them last week about hanging the sleeping bags on the tents to dry them'.

This made me suddenly realise that the Tax Partner was so often present when I was speaking to people that he didn't have much choice but to learn what was happening and he probably knew almost as much as me. I was also impressed that he was still keen to come out with me as often as it must have been fairly dull just hearing about preparation for the North Pole again and again, especially from someone so inexperienced.

The second way I determined to eat more was by helping myself more often to food in the kitchen. It was accepted that people would put bits of food there for everyone to eat on special occasions. Usually this would for birthdays, but it could be for anything. As a Partner I was previously always aware that people would watch what I was eating and I didn't not eat, but I had previously been careful and took a small piece whereas now I greeted this food with grace and ate a reasonable slice possibly going back for seconds. This got noticed but everyone put it down to the North Pole and I think, on occasions, brought more in.

I didn't appreciate it at the time but the local office were almost enjoying it as much as I was, and there was a sense of pride that they knew someone was going to the North Pole. In one case a new manager in our office went off to a recruitment day and he explained to me in front of several people how they had a quiz about the offices and Basingstoke had been ignored when they were going around the southern region. This annoyed us a bit because we often felt ignored, not because they were ignoring us but because we were too small to often be considered, but then he said the last question was which office has a partner going to the North Pole. He said that we didn't really think about it because I was always here but the real shock and joy that was apparent in the people from other offices was incredible. Straight after that quiz they went for a break and everyone was talking about it. He didn't know exactly how many got it right but he knew it was Basingstoke, how the training was going and also where the blog was on our internet sight.

I was becoming very aware that a lot of people were getting a measure of vicarious pleasure through knowing that I was going to the North Pole. This sense of feeling steadily increased throughout my training and the trip itself. I did have to force myself to remember this on the trip, although I never really thought of dropping out when I began to start having dark questions that was a very easy way of stopping them. Letting myself down was one thing but I couldn't let others down.

I continued going to the group training sessions and I was enjoying them because it was the only period I had with people who were actually going through the same stuff as me. To be fair, they were all much better suited to this than I was but that did not matter because the fact I wasn't suited to it was a lot of the reason I was going. The next event was now due and the activity was a walk for around three hours and covering ten miles. This was a nice event for me and I passed it accordingly. I was not actually sure if you could still fail but afterwards it was never an option for the organisers. The walk was fantastic. It was a reasonable stroll and it gave me a chance to speak to the other people on the trip. It was just before a large payment was due to the organisers and there were a lot more people than the next session so I suspect those people thought it was going to be too expensive. This was a shame, but you had to do what suited you and if they couldn't afford it then this was the right time to drop out. One person had come second in a national tough guy competition which didn't mean anything to me but apparently it is circuit training but extreme. He was a fun person and you have to feel he would have been very good.

This session was done a year before we were due to go, and the previous racers were running their first version of the race which inspired a lot of talk due to the failings of the race and they were effectively our opposition. They were not our opposition but we felt they were. More interestingly were the number of problems in their race. The most striking was someone who got frost bite on his penis, when the clip came out on television he had about two centimetres of body tissue frozen so it was not as bad as we thought but for us it was sort of funny but more importantly very scary. Several other racers had levels of frost bite on their hands and it seemed their training was insufficient. To be fair, when we met them at our race we could see nothing wrong with their race or racers so if there were problems they had resolved them by the second year.

The inside training again just emphasised the fact that you had to be sensible and there was also an element on attracting sponsorship for the race. We had to make sure we had a split between charity sponsorship which for me was really simple. I would not put any of that money against the cost of the trip so all charity money went to Anthony Nolan Ltd and the local Basingstoke trust. The second area was if you were getting the trip sponsored.

My situation was, I would have Baker Tilly or no one and Baker Tilly were unlikely to pay more than the trip cost so I didn't worry too much about this but some people seemed a bit worried. Being an Accountant, I offered to help anyone with this and I got a few conversations that afternoon but no one wanted formal help. By now I had got into the training at home and had a system of doing weights at home one day and walking round the park at the bottom of my road pulling a couple of car tyres. This looked incredibly stupid but did provide great training for the trip as it pulled on exactly the parts of the body the sled was going to pull on. It was quite funny in Winchester because I went at the same time, early in the morning and, when I went, I started seeing the same dog walkers but they looked at my sled and just ignored me. I think one said something when I had seen him for around a month.

The next session was in June and this was the session when we had to fill a form in saying who we wanted to be in the team with. This was very simple for me, the two I wanted to be with were obvious but if I couldn't do that I wasn't really bothered and I would go with anyone. It turned out the other two members were quite definite they wanted the three of us to form a team and so our team of Alex, Charlie and myself was formed.

The bulk of the session was to do with getting to understand the GPS and we had some example tents that we had to erect. It is quite incredible to think we would put them up in a bad wind in the Arctic in just a few minutes but at the training session, it took about thirty minutes, but it was just a routine and once you knew the routine it was a simple, all- important exercise.

Now that I had a team I felt committed and it meant that at future sessions I would be with my team more often than not, and I now had a particular identity. We would have to choose a name for our team and I e-mailed a few suggestions to the others and they liked Northern Stars. A partnership who joined the race together were the first to give their name of the Gentlemen Adventurers, it was an okay name but they were both doctors and instead of the flying doctors in Australia I had thought of the frozen doctors but probably, rightly, they thought that was tempting fate.

Although this period was effectively about reaching the North Pole I was still going to work, socialising and going to Round Table. During the summer the Euro 63 meeting was in Belgium and as usual, I went. I hadn't thought about this till I got there but I realised Finland would have snow before I went and it would be sensible to get some practice at cross country skiing, even if it would be more of heavy drinking than skiing. I decided to speak to Jerki as he, I felt, would turn me down the gentlest, but to my surprise he said "Leave it to me" and "I will speak to you again in about half an hour". He actually took about five minutes and he said "You need to come this week and we will go up to the Arctic Circle for a few days". This had also broken the news to Round Table and they all seemed very interested in it.

As was expected, Belgium was not the best of methods of keeping the training going but I knew about this before I left and I just had to fit this in, but at Round Table events you can expect there to be a lot of drinking, and being Belgium there was a lot of beer! The weekend soon went and we disappeared but I felt quite proud of myself for getting a skiing trip out of it.

At work I then had one of life's natural ironies. I was being sponsored for the Anthony Nolan Trust because of their connection with Round Table. I didn't know this but they were in fact a client of the Guildford office. We wanted to do a Strategic Planning Toolkit on them and they were a significant client and we were doing a charity specific toolkit for the first time so I was asked to do it. The toolkit took a weekend so we had a chance to talk in the evening and I mentioned I was going to the North Pole and raising money for them. Again they were ecstatic over this and asked me bring a flag with me for signature.

The next session proved the hardest for me in that it was climbing a hill but we were all tied together and typically there were five or six and we raced up and down the hill a few times. I did alright but I was clearly suffering by the end of the hill climb and was almost physically sick. My two team mates reacted just as I would have wanted in that they checked I was alright to which I said "Yes, but I need a few minutes to catch my breath" and then they left me to it. Charlie gave me some of his drink rather than let me drink my own water. Apparently it was some kind of energy drink; it tasted dreadful but certainly did the job. Having completed the hill climbs we then did a far simpler walk around the hillside and this proved one thing, I could walk even if the other activities were a problem.

Alex was talking at this session about pulling tyres around a park in London. He said it was getting difficult because everyone there wants to stop him and talk about the tyres and where he is going. He also mentioned that his girlfriend was slightly jealous at the female attention, although he was clearly joking but it reminded me about it taking a month or so before people said anything where I was. Well I suppose that is the difference between London and Winchester. This session was out in the West Country where one of the organisers lived and he would be looking after the daily rations. Each team had to take responsibility for getting the rations and we had a budget given to us by the organisers. I had agreed to get the rations for our team and foolishly though the budget was an actual limit rather than the amount we could knock off our bill. Being an Accountant really helped me in budgeting and preparing a forecast. In addition, I took a bit of advantage of the marketing team at work and spent a morning with the office marketing girl doing the shopping, and they took a few photographs.

It was incredible. I had spent around a couple of hundred Pounds but I had everything. The next stage was to weigh each item out and put it in bags, the only thing I would leave would be cutting the Mars bars until we were in the Arctic. Each bag was amazing. It had various dried fruit and an assortment of sweets including liquorice, chocolate and various standard sweets. I didn't think too much about them but when I gave them to the organiser he said they were the best bags he had seen.

One issue that annoyed me immensely and, not because she did it, but because of the stupidity of how she did what she did was when my current girlfriend ate sweets from the completed bags rather than from the unsorted section. I asked her if she had done that before and she said but didn't know which bags or sweets she had taken out. I had to re-weigh them all to find out which bags were affected and then re-weigh the sweets to replace them. To this day I can't work out why she took them from the completed bags when the unsorted sweets were there as well.

I had put liquorice in each bag before Alex had warned me that he didn't like the pure liquorice so before I gave them to the organiser I had to go through all of Alex's bags and extract the pure liquorice, weigh them out and replace them with the combined liquorice from the liquorice all sorts bags. Considering I had done approximately twenty five bags for him it was quite frustrating. I mentioned this to one of the other competitors but thought nothing about it. Then once we had finished the race he told me how impressed he was by this and that he thought what a great team member I was, unfortunately he told me with Alex there and I had to say I hadn't told Alex about it yet.

The next session was to be very exciting as they were going to give us our kit for the expedition. This was a hugely important issue for us as and, after this, we would have pretty much everything for the trip and it made me and I'm told, the others, feel that the trip was going to go ahead and more importantly with me. Most of the session was spent receiving the goods, most of which were individual and, although everyone had the same there were specific sizes of clothes.

As we tried everything on it looked wrong seeing people in the UK dressed for the North Pole especially as they were all jumping around with enthusiasm. After the clothes there were other items such as a GPS and the goggles but individually it was about just looking the part. We then had the team goods which we split fairly sensibly amongst us but the main item was the tent, which we had to erect to make sure it was all there. We were getting faster, but still nowhere as quick as we would have to be in the Arctic. Alex said he would take the tent which suited me as I would have found storing it difficult. I agreed to take the cooking equipment as I knew I would get involved with that. The cooking equipment was everything we would need except for the fuel which would be a lot cheaper in Canada and, more importantly, a lot safer than travelling half way around the world with it.

The main meals were still missing from our kit and included in this session was an eating session to choose what we would take. The items were military packs that just needed boiling water on them to make a variety of meals. Our team liked all of them except the rather strange mixed rice which was rice slightly flavoured in the bag. As a result we applied for equal goods of each thing except we didn't want the rice, unfortunately when the goods arrived so did the rice. Fortunately we had rations for about thirty days but could only expect to be on the ice around twenty days so we should be able to avoid eating the rice. We had one session early on before we were racing but did not have to have it again. Actually the main meals were very good although I don't know if they were or just that I was so hungry at the end of the day.

With the main meals we also had to arrange for a selection of breakfasts to take with us. I don't really remember these but there were three varieties of porridge, again these were fantastic at doing what they needed to do.

I was getting on fine with my training although I knew I was underweight for the trip but I was doing enough training. With work to go, I knew the goods were to be divided by three on the trip. That is until one day I got an email from Jock inviting me and my two team mates to London on Friday. Charlie had always stated that his work was going to pay for him and if he didn't get the money he wouldn't go. I was surprised it had not come up earlier but they hadn't paid and probably weren't going to pay. Unfortunately Charlie had to drop out that evening leaving me and Alex a two-man team but with a larger tent than we needed.

Alex and I were both very upset but we couldn't blame Charlie although we think that is why we got invited by Jock to try and bully Charlie into going. Charlie had told his wife he wouldn't pay their money to go and unfortunately that was that. Charlie went off early after that but we told him if work did pay there would be no problem with him re-joining us. Alex and I went off to find some dinner and talk.

We went to a club he was a member of and started talking. I don't remember much about the talk but there was one critical matter we discussed about tactics. I think it is fair to say we would not win a race over all four stages as there were people who were faster than us and we only had two people and three person's kit, well with the tent anyway. Although that was fair cop I explained to Alex that the first leg would probably be more subtle and about who was on the ice the most rather than how fast they went.

At the first check point people would find out how long each day people had been travelling but until that point they wouldn't know and if you left very early in the morning you could probably win. Alex said that I thought the first leg was about having the biggest balls to which I agreed. We each remembered this throughout the rest of the training and the first leg of the trip.

Back at work we had a southern area Partner's conference; these were always fairly fun as you got to meet Partners from the other offices in our region. This year would be interesting but I knew I couldn't make the national Partners conference that would be held in Madrid. This would be an interesting conference for me as I was missing the national partnership conference. I remember when they said where it would be, they had already announced the dates so I knew I couldn't go and I must have been the only person wishing it wasn't Madrid.

The national Chairman was at our conference and he started explaining why people were missing the main event which very few did and they had to give a good excuse and, more importantly, the excuses would be made public. He had said all the people not going without naming them and then "one person is going to the North

Pole". In the southern region everyone knew so gave no reaction which clearly shocked the Chairman a little bit.

As part of the conference we were split into five teams to discuss certain things and then for a member to report back to the conference. We were to discuss the fifth and most difficult item and I had been chosen to report back. The Chairman had done all the other regional conferences and made the point that no one had really sorted this matter out before we left for discussion. This was a lot to do with my team mates but the report was fantastic. Everyone else had got straight into the matter as there were only a few minutes to discuss it but we had developed a key starting point and from then on it was just to keep rolling.

At the end, the Chairman thanked me profusely and said that I would be presenting our findings at the national conference to which I said "only if you pull me back from the North Pole". I thought nothing more of this but it was clear the chairman was interested if he could pursue it further. After dinner, I was asked to go and have a chat with him about the North Pole. I said "We will probably have finished the first leg by the time of your conference and a direct call may be possible, but it would probably be safer for a fixed video to be done as there are several variables that are difficult to predict and it may be nothing will work". We agreed to a video and the possibility of a phone call but in the end just did the video.

I was driving through the countryside one day shortly after the conference when the phone rang and I looked at the call and it was from Charlie. The last time I had a call from Charlie was when he had to drop out of the race. Fortunately I was near a layby so I pulled up and took the call. Fantastic news, Charlie's firm had agreed to pay for him and he was back in the race. I was going with or without Charlie but there was no doubt it would be better and easier with him.

The organisers had decided the December session would be slightly lighter-hearted than normal and so we went and did the shooting practice. I was particularly bad at this but I knew if we saw a polar bear we would be aiming above it. The big thing I remember about this was it turned out we were on the land of David who was officially our race organiser even if it was Jock who did everything. During one person's shoot he was suddenly told to cease firing as David wandered through the rifle range but safely to join us. It was great to actually meet the man. The day was definitely a light-hearted event and we had a good lunch and did a bit more shooting and an easy identification exercise before leaving for home.

It was Christmas and as per usual I had agreed to go to Brighton and stay with my parents. This year both my sisters and their families would visit for dinner. Both my sisters also live in Brighton so it was just a question of whether it was her or her husband's year for visiting their family. I had received a warning from my eldest sister that all my mother wanted was a picture if me. I assumed it was in case I didn't return but I thought I should do this properly. When I knew this I had contacted a Round Table contact of mine. He had just left Table but I knew he was a good photographer and had his own photography business and asked him to take a portrait of me. He was, not surprisingly, willing to do so. He took my photo and we agreed on a particular picture using the magic of a digital screen. We then decided on a frame for it and he said it would be ready in two weeks. I collected the photograph two weeks later and he said that has wife's friends had been round and seen it and said it "sort of looks like David Aston". This was the first hint I had that I was putting on weight! I knew these women but didn't see them that often so it was interesting what they thought. I wrapped the photograph up and also bought my parents a clock and wrapped that up as well and took both identically looking wrapped presents to Brighton. I am afraid I then failed a bit because my parents opened the clock first as I hoped they would but couldn't then find the photograph. I had to search for the photograph which had got hidden behind the settee. When my mother opened it she was very impressed and said that was all she had wanted.

At an earlier session Jock had mentioned the problem with going to the Pole and having old style metal fillings in place. Normally there was no problem but it had been known that a person's fillings had frozen and, as he said, "you would know about it". I am afraid to say that I had five old fillings in place and I would do anything to stop them freezing up so I went to my local dentist and asked his opinion. He explained that the best way to avoid any danger was to take them out and to refill them with the best, most modern stuff. I suspect he did very well out of me but I couldn't choose to ignore him. The treatment probably took two months going to the dentist once or twice a fortnight. It left me in agony the night I went to the dentist but that pain soon disappeared and at least I knew I would be safe. I also got his assistant to take a few photographs of me having my teeth altered so that I could firstly remember what I had had to go through but secondly it would gave me something to add to my blog.

We had one last training session to go and it was a weekend in Wales in the middle of winter. This, on the face of it, was a horrific weekend but obviously I was getting into it more because I actually enjoyed it. The funniest thing on this trip was that Charlie had brought his special North Pole sleeping bag because it was give or take freezing outside. He was sweating awfully and in the end had to sleep with it open because it made him so hot.

The trip was a clear reminder of what we were going to have to do but it still failed to warn us about the fact that you had to deal with the night at the end of a day's trekking. This is what I found the hardest. When you stopped walking you had to put the tent up, cook and anything else before sleeping and taking down the tent to start again. It was the middle of February and as cold a time of year as anytime so it seemed a good idea to go to Finland. I had also not been drinking since the New Year celebrations and I knew I could not visit Jerki, Juha and their friend without having a few drinks. Still, I knew this at Christmas. Giving up drink would be a good idea and I would just have to make the Finland trip a programmed gap in that arrangement.

Finland was everything I had dreamed it would be. It was largely a booze-up but the Finns knew what it was about and they did make sure there was enough skiing particularly on the four days we went to stay in the Arctic circle. Whilst we did lots of skiing and I at least got used to wearing them they made sure that it was fun as well with a variety of different exercises. The one I remember most was having done a reasonable ski in the morning the afternoon we went for a walk but on our skis. I didn't really understand why we had our skis on but they just said you might not be able to ski everywhere at the pole and I believed them. We didn't go too far but they were obviously giving me a taste of the different conditions. At one point I had Jerki's fitness watch and he was amazed when he saw how little my heart rate had risen. He actually said for the first time he knew I could do the trip.

At the end of this trip they then challenged me to take off my ski's and told me then I would know why I had kept them on. I did so and it was amazing. I suddenly fell down beyond my knees in the snow.

The next day was similar we did a cross country ski in the morning around a pre-set path of around twenty kilometres again stopping at the café at the end if the route for lunch but more importantly for their hot apple punch. I expect in a normal day in the absence of any skiing it would taste awful but at the end of a morning skiing and a lot of falling down and getting up again it was fantastic.

In the afternoon we went out on jet skis and I was the passenger although my driver kept changing. This was a more stressful afternoon than I had imagined. They were clearly all very experienced and knew how to ride them although there was a time when Jerki took a corner too sharply and just went straight off. We tried to get back ourselves but the snow was too deep so we had to wait until someone realised and turned back to find us.

One evening we were there we decided to go to a night club which amused me because I believed I had been everywhere for about ten miles and I had seen no club. They agreed with me, they said they were going to the nearest club but it is forty miles away. I felt sorry for Juha because he drove but apparently it was just his turn.

Wherever I went and whoever I saw it was all getting very Pole-related. I couldn't believe how excited people were. It was March and I would leave at the end of the month. At work I had either brought work forward or got it pushed back so I had five weeks free. Whenever I went to clients they wanted to know when I was going and what I was expecting to find and when I tried talking accounts they weren't interested.

It was in this last month they I arrived at work one morning to find a handwritten Baker Tilly envelope on my desk. It was the first and I think the last time I had a hand written Baker Tilly envelope. I opened it before I did anything else and I realised there was a cheque for more than they had originally told me. To be honest, I had thought they had decided not to fund me as I had heard nothing since it was first mentioned right at the beginning. Anyway, I was ecstatic that they offered to pay as much as they did. I decided to give the Regional Manager a call when the offices were open and, to my great surprise, he was delighted to speak to me and he also said he was coming to my farewell from the firm in my last week.

I had decided I would have to keep things tight for the North Pole as I had expected to have to borrow a bit but now with Baker Tilly paying me for the trip I could buy a few extras. Most notably was a camera. I went to a proper camera shop in the middle of Winchester and, whilst he may have known about cameras, he knew nothing about the North Pole. When I arrived I said I want a camera for the North Pole. It had three needs; it must have a battery that is charged separately from the camera so someone else can charge a battery whilst I am travelling. It needs to be made of plastic so it doesn't freeze up and it has to have a screen which will not freeze up. The moment I said that he picked up a metal camera, then when I told him it was metal and I didn't want metal he picked up one where to charge the battery needed the camera. Eventually he listened to me and stopped selling me a camera in the normal way of telling me what it was good at and gave me a camera and said this will survive the Pole. I gave it a quick look through and bought it. The camera is still going strong and it is fantastic. It does far more than I will ever need.

In the last couple of weeks I guess I did some work but I don't remember any. Again I had a run of the local television, radio and newspaper to do. By now I had become quite good at the media and I was able to join in the fun and make jokes about where I was going. Perhaps the most memorable was when I did the breakfast radio for a local station but I was getting interviewed by Maggie Philben. When I was a child she was on Multi Coloured Swapshop which I watched most Saturday mornings. It was a few years on from then but I was fully aware of who she was.

During the last week the firm had decided I should do a farewell presentation. They invited the usual people but they suggested I also invite my parents. I was going to do most of the talking about how I had got ready but I was very lucky and also managed to get Jock down from London to talk about why he organised the race.

I had also decided to try videoing this presentation and I persuaded a couple of the mangers to take a video for me. They were delighted by this as it meant a couple more of the team could enter the talk. Usually no-one wanted to go from our team next door and they all had to be pushed into it but for this time everyone wanted to go. My parents and, my mother in particular, were not truly enamoured with me going on the trip and had decided I wasn't coming back. I do believe them coming to this event and hearing Jock speak put their minds at rest a little bit even if I did find them sitting in the middle of the front row off-putting. In addition, to them I had the top Partner in the region there as well so it was quite intimidating but as I have always said just be sensible and no-one can argue with you.

Jock as always was quite amusing and candid with what he said but the real event was down to me. I think the event went well; it is difficult to say because it was not the same as a usual seminar. The main thing was my parents and the Regional Partner enjoyed it.

The last week I had to pack after having done a day at work. I packed everything and ticked it off at least twice but I made sure I had everything. Fortunately I did have everything as I dread to think what would have happened if I had missed any item. This was so different for me, normally I check I have my tickets, my wallet and my keys but everything was done to the last detail. As I say, I spent a week packing just to be sure. I checked my weight the night before I left. I had given myself a target of ten stone but unfortunately I fell short of that. However, as my Body Mass Index was just below twenty but I was clearly as heavy as I had ever been and this was a vast improvement on normal so I will just have to make this work for me.

3   Acclimatisation

The morning when we were due to fly out arrived and I
had everything ready so I could head off. I went early
because the girl I was seeing had got the morning off but
they wanted her to do the afternoon. To be honest, I was a
nervous wreck and would probably have torn the house
down. I couldn't check in until the others arrived as we
had team kit to take but I arrived mid-morning and we
were due to fly much later.

I stayed at Heathrow and waited for the others to arrive. It
appeared a lot had the same idea as me and it was not
long before a few others had arrived and they all seemed
just as nervous and equally as excited as me. Eventually
everybody had arrived and we set about checking in. We
had all our kit and so our baggage allowance was sixty
kilograms and that was just about alright but stuff needed
to be equalled out across us. We eventually got sorted out
and checked in.

We had done everything we needed to and so had a
couple of hours to wait before we took off so my team
decided to go for dinner. It was quite strange eating for
the first time with them both knowing what was coming
next. Charlie told us he was in trouble from his wife for
going because she had just found out she was pregnant, to
which I said "you should be back in time". It wasn't really a
joke but Alex found it hilarious and kept laughing at it

which frankly unnerved me a bit as I knew I had five weeks with him in a tough environment and pretty much he would be visible to me at all times.

The flight itself was relatively quiet as firstly we were split up and secondly everyone was a touch nervous. As we were about to land Jock came round and told us all that we had no food to declare because it had all been agreed before. I did as I was told and ticked no food on the import card and then signed it. I have never done this before or since and I was worried at customs but I went through without any problems. It made me think I know I have my thirty bags of food plus some of the team dinners so surely I should declare it.

We had one night in Ottawa and we decided to get some extra food before the entire group went to a restaurant. We walked up the road to a local convenience store which had a delicatessen and ordered some dried beef to add to the bags which they sold to us and we all thought this was fantastic. In the race we were all sick at some point and we don't know but suspect this may not have been a good buy. After this, we went to the restaurant as a group which was all right but I just wanted to go to sleep and it went on and on. Anyway, we got back to the hotel and I slept.

The next day we were going to fly to Resolute Bay but before that I could have a hotel breakfast and I was determined to have as much as possible before travelling.

We all met up for breakfast and one of the female team members was asking them about what coffee they had and then picked up some maple syrup and asked for that. The funny thing was rather than just saying that's not coffee they made a real fuss about it. I ate as much as I could because we didn't know when we would have a proper meal again.

It made me realise just how far Resolute Bay was and how quiet it is there as I grabbed a newspaper available for Canadian residents and looked at the weather reports. The forecast only went as far as Iqaluit in the north. At the time I didn't know where that was but later that day I realised it was about half way to Resolute Bay from Ottawa and completely ignored on the national forecast maps.

We all got together to fly to Resolute Bay, I didn't realise but it was a two-stage flight stopping at Iqaluit and then going on to Resolute Bay. The flight assistants were obviously used to the dangers of the trip and spoke freely about them. I had a seat next to the wing so I had to help if the plane crash landed. She told me to follow the yellow line and help people off but, if I was scared, to run and leave the people to find their own way off!

As the flight took off they started bringing drinks around but kept stopping for a few minutes and one of our group asked them why they kept stopping. She just winked at him and said "because the weather is bad". The flight kept on like this until we eventually made Iqaluit. At Iqaluit we were forced to get off as we were taking another plane up to Resolute Bay. We were effectively stranded in a hut until the plane was ready, I think about two hours. I read every sign in this hut and particularly the ones about polar bears. Instead of just saying be careful they had lots of different warnings. I liked two in particular; one saying that you could get kiiled and the other you could get eaten.

We then took off for Resolute Bay and this flight was relatively uneventful but it made me realise how white the area was. I thought we were above the clouds but we were actually below them and it was just white. On arrival at Resolute Bay our stuff was moved into the base camp and we were then taken for a short walk around the village. It was very cold and I was glad I was wearing the right kit, particularly the jacket. The short walk made me realise just how small the village was. As part of the walk we met several Inuit children who thought we were mad but were delighted we saw where they lived. Resolute Bay is interesting because some people who live there are actually paid to do so by the Canadian Government and hence are actually quite rich but also have to live there for a period of time.

The view of Resolute Bay was quite interesting but I had to concentrate on the pole and getting all our kit and in particular the food together. The remainder of the week would be quite a lot outside but the time inside was actually just as important. That night we slept in the base camp and then ate breakfast there which was a real treat because we knew what was coming. We then got together as a complete group and went outside, this time to practise skiing and in particular cross country skiing. My time in Finland had done some good but a week is only a week and unsurprisingly I was still very bad at skiing. I got better as the trip went on but I have to admit that I was quicker walking than skiing. We spent a couple of hours doing this and trying to climb a small hill outside the base camp. I just about climbed it, but not without falling over a few times and then it was back to the base camp to begin getting all our kit together.

We began having tutorials every day where everyone went but it was funny how team-based they became, particularly when we had been on walks and every team had their own findings from the walk. After the skiing we had our first tutorial and, without saying it, it was obvious that each team was making their fellow team members sound fantastic when clearly a lot weren't. My skiing was bad but I wasn't the worst. However, even the worst were all right according to their team. The tutorials were good as it meant, despite the biased nature of events, we got to know how the teams were doing.

People were gradually becoming aware of the teams different approach to the race and it was quite clear when one of the male contenders wanted to win and most people expected him to as he was prepared to do anything to win. My team wanted to do as well as possible but we knew we would find it very difficult. The first leg was our secret and we were still determined to win it. It was also clear that the winners ought to be the two doctors but they were too happy playing around. Once they started to race they would win the races but although this was clear I couldn't tell them because it would ruin our plan for the first leg.

We went for another group walk the next day but this day was more about what we do on the ice and we erected the tents and got all the kit out. It was amazing that finding where the kit went was very difficult but equally very important. It was beginning to dawn on me that getting to the North Pole was probably more about coping when you are not moving then actually travelling to the North Pole. This is an area I completely missed and I needed to get up to speed with this as soon as possible. Asking the other members about this it appeared this had, to some extent, been missed by the others as well.

The afternoon was spent quite frivolously in and around the tents with all the teams within a short distance of each other, although it was fun and frivolous it is quite frightening to think how important the tent layout had become. I realised, well it confirmed, the others were far stronger than me and it did make me realise I should offer to cook for the entire trip if they would agree to take a bit more stuff. They didn't have much choice but they accepted and the fact I offered showed I was trying to help and get the team there as fast as possible.

In the evening at the base camp I realised I had left my hat in the tent and decided I would go and get it without borrowing anyone else's because the tent was only fifty yards away. This seemed a perfectly good plan to me and even the fact that a local Inuit child was looking at me like I was an idiot didn't persuade me to not go. In fact, I went away laughing to myself about the child. Wow was the child correct! I don't know the temperature but it was very cold and I mean very cold. I got into the tent as fast as possible, found the hat and returned. Putting the hat on immediately made an ear burn. I knew that actually was good as I had a bit of frost nip and it was now thawing out. I couldn't believe it but it was a very good lesson for me. Frost nip is the stage before frost bite and it was beginning to become frost bite but could easily be cured at that stage, although it does need attention.

The day had arrived where we were going to sleep outside for the first time. This hadn't been a problem for me before but now that we actually had the tent up, even with our sleds outside we had everything we needed inside and for three people it looked very small. At one end of the tent I was using it as the kitchen and the other end we came in and out and left our boots there but took the inside of the boots with us. That left the inner body of the tent for everything else and especially everyone had to survive in it.

We were about to go to sleep and I realised how light it was. You could tell the sun had gone down and it was dark. Although I had a head light with me, you would only need it for technical work and not for anything else and it was getting brighter every day. I thought I might need the head torch on leg one but probably not after that. I would have a look at whether or not I would take it nearer the time. I was working out a strategy both individually but, more importantly, with the team as well. As we were about to sleep I decided to hang up my gloves. Firstly, the tent had four pieces of cord around the roof. This would probably not be thought of for use but they were there and the tent was very small so if it existed, use it. Secondly, I thought nothing of this. We had a carabineer come with the gloves so I hung it up but both Alex and Charlie were amazed by this. They had seen the carabineers with the gloves but thought they were a flash marketing trick and thrown them away. Fortunately I had, for some reason, brought a couple of carabineers I had at home and they were very welcome into the tent kit list.

I slept reasonably well but did wake up a few times. Never anything serious and never for very long but I did realise that. What was of more concern was the lesson I learnt in the morning. It was incredible how long everything took. Firstly I couldn't find the matches to cook, when I found them I couldn't get them alight. Eventually we managed to get one to light and the fuel was alight for the cooking but it took a lot longer than usual. The fuel was alight but I realised I had no water, there was plenty of snow but you need a bit of water to get it going. Fortunately Alex had not quite finished his and I got going. About fifteen minutes later Charlie asked if it was ready but it wasn't. I had the guards around the hob pieces correctly so the flame went straight up and was contained in but I hadn't put the lids on the saucepans. I put them on and we eventually got enough boiling water to have one of our porridges for breakfast. Some people had given up on cooking and went inside for breakfast. I am not sure if that was good or not. Clearly it was better food but I had learnt several huge lessons. Not only about the cooking but also what I had to keep warm and hence keep on me including at night.

We had all been given urine bottles so that we could go to the loo when we were in the tent. I slept with mine and it was ok the next morning. I don't know why I did but I did. This was good because one person left his in the tent but outside of his sleeping bag and it froze up. Fortunately he was near the base camp and able to defrost it relatively easily but this was another lesson we learnt.

We were going on a long walk before setting off properly on the race so we decided we would get up reasonably early and head off so we could get settled in as soon as possible. We woke up early in the morning, packed up the tent and were ready to leave. Before we went we decided to have a team photograph taken by the organisers. We still don't know how we missed it but apparently everyone had agreed to start a bit later but we missed that. Once you've packed up you have to go so it was a bit sad but we just had to go.

It was a good morning getting ready to go. I was beginning to understand how the cooking worked; I kept matches on me overnight so they were warm enough to light the units. I understood how the lighting guards worked and sent flames upright. Most importantly, I now understood to keep water to start the snow boiling and I now remembered to put the lids on saucepans. This walk was pretty much like a day on the race as we had almost all the stuff with us except for a bit of fuel and some of the food. Despite this I seemed to have a good day and kept up with Charlie and Alex. The walk was, however, very good and we got back and settled into the camp. A bit later on the South African team came back and they looked rough. Alex had spotted them and made Charlie and I look.

I had bought a load of hot chocolate and coffee from the UK but we had now decided that we wanted hot chocolate alone on the trip and so I had to get some extra hot chocolate. In order to complete this we went to the supermarket to acquire it. They had the hot chocolate so we bought it but it was Canadian and not British hot chocolate. I packed this not thinking anything about it.

Back at the camp was the last chance we had to ensure everything was packed except for tomorrow morning which was going to be cutting it fine. As I would be the cook I was getting all the food packed. I still couldn't understand it but everyone wanted to see my lunch bags thanks to some great talking about them by one of the organisers. He said they were very happy when Charlie dropped out because one third of these bags could become the organiser's rather than having to buy their own and when Charlie was back in, they lost this opportunity. Anyway, if people wanted to see them they could.

Another factor was the work carrier bags, I had a delivery of one hundred before I left because we were going to have our feet wrapped in them for walking but we subsequently decided against this. Little did we know that carrier bags were like gold dust and once we had used all we needed the four-man team asked for the remaining bags. I was, of course, delighted for them to have them. Particularly as one of the girls in the team had given us all a face mask before starting which was in addition to the standard kit but frightfully useful.

I got all of the food packed up for each leg as requested. Fortunately, we had over stocked on these items because of the spare days we had to allow for bad weather. So, I packed these carefully and hoped we won't need them. I had also come with a large amount of wet wipes. Before I came I wasn't really sure why I had bought them but they had been mentioned as useful. Once I arrived and begun camping the use of them was obvious. Firstly we could use them to wash ourselves as far as possible, clearly it was not as good as a genuine wash but it was far easier, took up a lot less luggage and most importantly they were safe.

Alex and Charlie were doing the other last minute changes to the kit. We had already stuck the tent poles together so that they were already partly done each evening and we didn't have to fold them away the next morning. This was simple but brilliant, I probably would never have thought of it but I don't know why not, but it saved us a lot of trouble although they did get frozen up from time to time.

We had been given a large supply of medical tablets because of where the trip was. With the other racers in the team they got the kit together before we were due to sleep and we were ready or so I thought. The team had been getting very friendly with one of the organisers. Alex was an ex-territorial army person and was experienced with tablets and, whereas we were told to try and remember which tablets did what, he also remembered what each of them looked like if they fell out of their packaging. I was extremely impressed with this.

One last tip we had been given is that the North Pole is in fact a desert and, therefore, the air is incredibly dry. This seemed amazing because when you are asked to think of deserts you would be expected to think of hot areas of the world and not of one of the coldest. Because it is a desert with dry air it is extremely good for drying things, providing the weather was alright for them being outside. This proved incredibly useful for drying the sleeping bags. We didn't know it but they made us sweat each night and absorbed our sweat. They shrunk in terms of outer width because of this but a couple of hours on the tent brought them right back to normal.

It was the last night before the race and as far as I was concerned we had everything ready and we should just get a good night's sleep. Some of the other teams were throwing a party and I agreed to go but very briefly. I stayed about twenty minutes and then went back to our room and tried to force myself to get some sleep. I couldn't get to sleep but at least I was in my bed not doing anything I shouldn't whereas some people were at the party and getting wasted. Charlie and I thought Alex was still at the party but instead he was talking to the organiser and getting some advice on improving our speed and also on minimising space. In terms of improving our speed this included things like only half putting a tent up if you are planning on leaving without sleeping. If you have to stop because you are snowed in or to have a meal before continuing, don't bother putting snow on the tent. You would be awake in the tent so would realise if anything is happening.

In terms of speeding the trip up this was simply a case of getting everything down as small as possible. The obvious example was the brush we had for sweeping out the tent each morning had a handle which he cut off as we didn't need it. I think this was probably a mistake but never mind.

The next morning came and we made sure we had a particularly strong breakfast as we weren't sure when we would have another. Everyone was talking about the race but before the race we had to be weighed and then go to a pre-race ceremony at the local restaurant. I was weighed and Jock laughed when he weighed me but also said that they would get me there.

We then went to the local restaurant for about mid-day. This was probably quite a useful ceremony for us all but I was thinking we could be racing now, particularly because the weather had started changing for the worse. The ceremony included an Inuit and her grandmother doing some throat singing. The most incredible thing about this was that the child looked about twenty and the grandmother about forty.

We were given a selection of vegetables for dinner that were probably incredibly difficult to get at the Arctic and probably very expensive but I kept seeing burgers and chips being ordered by the locals and I have to confess I would far rather have eaten those.

The last bit of the ceremony was a poem which Jock read to us. He finished it eventually and then we went off to the race at about half past one. Jock did take the opportunity to remind us of one useful tip in that wherever you are you have three warm points on your body and they are your two armpits and your crotch. We should not be surprised if a colleague has hands down his trousers as he is probably just keeping warm! I didn't really think about this after I finished the race until recently.

As a result of the stroke I am probably three or four degrees colder than I was and I can assure you that the armpits and occasionally the crotch have had some important use.

4   Leg 1

The race itself was divided into four legs. The intention of this was to make sure everyone got to the North Pole regardless of how suited to getting there they were. This suited me as I would need all the help I could get but it clearly didn't suit some of the other teams. My prime concern was the first leg and my personal belief was that we could win this leg even if we were unable to win any more. The distance was around fifty five miles which was a great distance to get started with. It was not a long distance by any means but it was far enough to get us into the race and it taught us a lot about travelling to the North Pole whilst giving us a decent stop at the end of the checkpoint.

At the start of the race lots of locals saw us off, which I didn't really think about at the time but it was actually quite good of them. They sang several songs which again, I don't really remember, as I was too busy weather-watching. The acclimatisation week had been on the whole comparatively good weather. Of course it was cold but it wasn't windy and there wasn't an actual storm but this race had just started and a storm was brewing. This was bad news for all of us but it was the same for us all and we just had to get on with it.

At the start we were all together and we followed the others along the standard route although what we saw was a team were actually going over land and taking a different route. Alex asked if we should follow them and Charlie said "no, leave them to it" so unfortunately we lost sight of them fairly early on. When we next saw them they said they had gained about a mile but it didn't look too good a track to be following.

We stopped after the first hour as per our original plan and everyone checked everyone's faces too see if they had the start of frost bite. We were more careful with this than ever before or ever after. I suspect this was a bit due to the fact that the weather had declined so much and a bit because we were now racing and had no base camp if there was a problem. Anyway there was no such problem and with a bit of my food bags inside us we were able to carry on. We remembered our chat the day Charlie thought he had dropped out and we recalled, to win this leg; we just had to spend more time on the ice rather than camped up. This was very difficult as the weather had got very nasty and everything was taking that much longer to do, but at least we knew the others would also be feeling this so we kept our fingers crossed and as far as possible stuck to our plan.

We decided, well when I say we decided, I mean Alex suggested and everyone else agreed. Alex was effectively our team leader, although he hadn't been appointed or stood for election we knew Alex would make most of the decisions then Charlie and last of all me. We were happy with this and the team I would say worked fairly well together considering we had never met except for the trip. Alex suggested we went across some land which was a bit of a shock but the wind wasn't quite as bad that way so we followed his lead.

This was good in terms of the race as it protected us quite a lot from the wind but what we began to notice was every so often an orange blob would appear. At the time we didn't see this as a problem but ultimately we realised it was off the front of Alex's sleigh. Every time he hit a bump his sled would stall and he would trim a very slight amount off which could prove to be a disaster. It hadn't happened yet, but it could do. It was Charlie who picked this up and he did seem worried. We ultimately decided to pack up for camp that day. We were satisfied with how far we had got, but only just. We knew that if the weather remained like this for the next day we would need an extra day for this leg but nature was going to make the decision.

The second day we were in the routine. At least, we thought we were. I am not sure what the others felt but I actually never felt I had got into the routine although I did get better. The second day we just kept walking although the weather was still bad and we did have to half put the tent up at one point because we couldn't see where we were going or, to the point, each other. Putting the tent up is a pain because even though we didn't place snow on the outside it is amazing how much work is required. It probably took as long to put up and take down as we stopped inside, but it had to be done. The one brilliant thing about the tent going up is that we had a cup of hot chocolate. I have never liked hot chocolate as much as I did on the trip. We probably lost about three hours but then carried on for a bit before stopping for the night. Again, Alex and Charlie did the tent work outside while I saw to the dinner, but first did a hot chocolate for everyone.

The next day we should have finished this leg but because of the bad weather we were going to be a day late. The truth of this dawned on us that night because we just weren't going as fast as we did in training as everything had to effectively be done twice due to the weather. Still, it didn't matter as we were sure it had affected everyone in the same way.

The third day arrived and I felt awful. I awoke at the normal time but I didn't want to get up. Eventually, I managed to force myself up but I didn't feel right. I cooked breakfast well enough but I knew this was going to be an extremely tough day. I managed to get myself ready for the normal time and we left as per usual but I was not right. I don't know what was wrong but I was definitely not right. This got worse the further we went. Despite my comments earlier I would willingly have stopped at any point on this day and I wouldn't have worried about winning the leg but I had two team mates and they had other ideas. My condition wasn't lost on them but I felt ill.

Eventually they decided we had gone far enough, and boy did I agree. I was absolutely useless when we stopped moving and I just gave up. I managed to get the hot chocolate drinks for the team, but I was a wreck and Alex very kindly offered to do the food. I am not sure Alex and Charlie realise how much I needed them then and gratefully they delivered without comment. Charlie asked me what was happening and, to be fair, I didn't know but, thanks to the two of them, we got past it eventually.

We decided we would get up at two o'clock the next day and make a dash for the first checkpoint. We believed we were still in with a shout but wouldn't know until we got there. All I wanted to do was go to sleep and I went pretty much straight away although I do remember someone asking "what were you thinking about on the ice?" Both Alex and Charlie went on for ages about their women, ideal food and a list of things. Then it came to me and all I could think of was left, right, left, right. They both laughed at this but we all knew that was exactly what I thought.

I fell asleep and hoped to be fast asleep until two o'clock when I would begin getting up but, as was the norm on this trip, nothing would go to plan. I awoke at about twelve thirty and I felt a bit odd. I was used to waking during the night but only for a few seconds but this was different. I felt weird and I didn't know why. Then suddenly and from nowhere I had the urge to be sick. I just made it to the boot room at the end of the tent. Importantly, the ground was pure ice and not the tent lining in the main room. My boots were on one side and the others the other side. I just managed to get my boots over and then I was sick twice. The one good thing about the freezing cold is at least the vomit froze quickly and there was no smell in the tent, but that was more luck than judgement and I probably should have attempted to get fully outside but I wasn't dressed for the occasion! If the other two realised they were just going to put up with it, but as per usual they both did.

I went back to sleep with the alarm set for two o'clock. I actually managed to get up at this time and, because I was cooking, I was the first up. The other two would be fifteen or so minutes later. Instead of returning to the cooking end I went to the other end and was sick again. This was most unfortunate, but at least it was on the other pile and again it froze. I decided to close my eyes for a few seconds to get over the fact I had just been sick. I closed them and they stayed shut. I awoke from this couple of seconds an hour and a half later at three thirty. Three thirty wasn't two o'clock but the other two weren't up and we all had alarms, so I felt a bit bad, but three thirty was still early and probably before anyone else which at the end of the day is what mattered. I got the breakfast ready and got the other two up. No one said anything about the time probably because they actually knew about me so I just got on with it. We set off on our dash for the pole and unfortunately I still felt bad and the weather had not improved yet. This was going to be another tough session but hopefully it would finish around midday. We went along as per yesterday and, whilst I was aware that Alex and Charlie were talking to each other, I was the same as yesterday and just kept thinking left, right, left, right. At one point I was sent ahead, I didn't really know why but I have since worked it out. The two of them were checking to see whether I had hyperthermia or not. I think they thought I did but it wasn't too bad so they carried on.

The first checkpoint was an old mine with an airport and the checkpoint would be placed just by the airport. We got to the airport and, to our relief, we saw no sled marks or ski marks so we were guessing no one was here yet, but we also saw no checkpoint. The weather was still bad and visibility was low so it could be close but where was it? Alex came up with the idea of splitting up to find it. I stayed on top of the hill with all the stuff and the other two left. It felt like ages but, after a couple of minutes, Alex returned and knew where it was. We grabbed Charlie and ran to the checkpoint. When we arrived the organisers got out of the tent to greet us and, more importantly, no one was in the tent. We had arrived first and won the first leg! It was truly amazing and even now I don't really believe it! Three other teams arrived within the next few hours but, it didn't matter, we had won the race. We were sitting talking to the race organisers and my illness came up. It was decided that while Alex and Charlie put the tent up I would go with the organiser to the medical tent and just sit there for a while. This was particularly good, not because it made me feel better although it did, but because I saw how they were using the lighting guards used for the cooking, but had split them up and were reflecting heat into the tent.

I was probably in there about an hour and there were two other racers from other teams who came in as well just to make sure. It was probably the best site at the checkpoint for the first hour or so but I vowed when I left the tent, it would be the last time I saw that tent.

The best thing about getting to the checkpoint at the front of the group was that we had some time there. For people like me, this was very important as it meant I could recover and get better before heading off again. For other people it felt like a waste of time, but it had always been this way. Nonetheless, one team was livid and wanted us to have a day at the checkpoint and then start on leg two but I loved having a break. I must have looked really ill because everyone kept asking me how I was feeling the first day but on the second day they all said how wonderful I looked. It is amazing what a bit of sleep does for you! Whilst we were at this camp we were able to swap the things we had used with new ones from the base came, so we now had a new set of food and fuel and gave the base camp our used photographs and camera battery and got brand new ones to start again.

I didn't know it for another few weeks, but the girl I was seeing at the time had decided when I said we would win the first leg that I genuinely meant it and had taken it to heart. She had actually had a bet at work that I would win the first leg and had clearly managed to win it. The prize was a pint at lunch every day until I returned so she was happy with me. She was also apparently very assertive when it came to exercising the prize.

It was at checkpoint one where I saw a polar bear in the wild for the first and last time. One of the race organisers had been made aware of this by the camp huskie and was watching it very carefully. I could just see a black point which I assume was his nose a couple of hundred yards away. The organiser pointed the gun in the air and fired. The noise scared the polar bear and that was as much of one as I saw. I still regret it a little bit but, the truth is, I didn't really want to see one at all.

We did hear at the break that in the team of four, two boys and two girls, one of the men had not been good at all. He had caught frostbite on one of his fingers and then managed to refreeze the finger again which is very dangerous. In addition to that, he had the gun tied into his sled and managed to drop it somewhere. They had no choice but to go back across their routes until they found it. This must have been soul destroying particularly as the weather at this stage was terrible.

Also, whilst on our break between legs, we tried what we had been told regarding the sleeping bags on the tent. We had all three sleeping bags out of the tent and tied them on to the roof not really expecting to get any results from it but the results were, frankly, amazing. We couldn't believe it, they went on the tent with lots of sweat inside but after a couple of hours they were back to their pre-pole state.

We had rested up and recuperated reasonably well so we were ready to go with the second leg. The weather had now improved dramatically and we now had good weather for the next few days. In addition, the days were longer now and we would not need any type of light to work by. It was still obvious when the sun had gone down, but it would still be visible and so even at midnight it just looked like early evening.

5   Leg 2

Leg two was our longest leg at about one hundred and twenty miles but it was on sea ice for a fair part of the way. There was a bay that we would get to and, because there was a rumour that the ice here hadn't set properly, everyone agreed in a meeting that we would come in to the coast and not be more than one hundred metres off the coast but that was the only dangerous part of the route.

As was the way, the leg started in the early afternoon. I never understood this. Why didn't they start in the early morning and give us a chance of properly attacking the first day? Still, it started when it started and we just had to put up with it. I suspect the organisers felt that there was perpetual daylight now so it didn't matter but I couldn't go on through the night and still be sensible the next day.

Being on sea ice meant it was best to pick a straight route and just follow it. This meant all the teams were just following each other as there was not a huge difference in the routes taken. In a lot of cases, if someone was ahead of you, it was possible to tell as their routes would still be showing in the form of walking or skiing and most importantly the sled.

The first day everyone was together apart from the three South Africans who formed the Ikey's team named after where they went to college, even though it was a good twenty or thirty years ago. They had had trouble on leg one and so they arrived late at the checkpoint and it was decided to stop them at the checkpoint for an extra day whilst we went ahead. This didn't seem totally fair but we were technically in a race and it meant they were a long way behind so I felt it was excellent if unfair.

The first day highlighted what I thought in that the race contenders were all noticeably quicker than we were, but we had the ability to stay on the ice a lot longer. As a result, we overtook all the teams towards the end of the day as they were camped up and ready and we went to bed that night very happy as we knew it was a case of getting out there and staying out there. In the first leg we had all skied everywhere because we knew it was the fastest route but, by the second leg, people were thinking of just walking. I tried this on day two. We found I was a lot better at keeping up with the other two in my team, partly because I was not wasting time to get food. If I wanted food I could just undo my zips and take the food without having to stop to grab the food.

It was clear I was the most unfit of all the racers but I knew that I could walk to ensure I retained as much fitness as possible but also I could keep going reasonably well. Above all, I was determined. So, as on the previous days, the others had overtaken during the day but come the end of the day, we walked past their tents as they camped for the night. We eventually stopped and were very happy with our positon and this stage, although as we slept that night, it all went horribly wrong for us.

The next day I got up and started cooking breakfast, but something was wrong. Alex was still sleeping and despite my attempts to wake him he was still asleep. Charlie had awoken and he said we better leave Alex alone until he wakes up naturally. Alex stayed asleep whilst I prepared the breakfast for Charlie and I and I could easily provide Alex's breakfast as and when he emerged. Whilst we knew this was going to delay us, we still felt that we would get going eventually. The fact is, at this stage, I was quite happy with being able to delay the start a little bit.

Alex eventually woke up an hour or so later and it was quite incredible how ill he actually looked. He said he was going to try sleeping longer and he didn't expect he would move at all today. He took the phone and rang back to the base camp with his illness. I was quite pleased, it sounded like food poisoning but the main thing was the camp doctor was confident that he would be fine tomorrow. We had probably lost any chance of winning the race but actually this meant we would no longer keep pushing ourselves as hard as we could.

Having an unexpected day's rest was actually fantastic for me and I slept quite a bit of it and I also managed to do some reorganisation of my things which made me feel a little better and improved the tents administration for the future. You would think it would be incredibly boring stuck in a tent in the middle of nowhere, but actually there was plenty to do. If it went on, it probably could become boring, but I was quite pleased with it.

The next day Alex was back to normal and it was quite a transformation. I had expected him to get up and be ready to move but I had not anticipated quite as dramatic a change. He was ready now and we needed to make sure we were ready as well. We got up and started travelling again, although no one said it, we had all decided we couldn't win the race.

There was a point in the race where you had to stay within one metre of the land base as a satellite showed there was potentially thin ice at sea. As we approached that area, we noticed that one team had gone straight on and ignored this. I can understand why they were tempted to do this but I wouldn't have gone anywhere near potentially thin ice deliberately. Fortunately, they got away with it but why take that sort of risk? We now had a usual travelling position of Charlie, then me with Alex following behind. In this position Charlie suddenly fell over with his sled falling into a gap near some ice furniture. Following Charlie I stopped and scooped his sled out of the whole and carried on. It was later I realised I had got some ice down my glove. It gradually warmed up in my glove as I was active, but then when I stopped it refroze and caused frostbite on my hand. It was very minor and never going to cause my hand, or at least part of it, to fall off but it grabbed my attention.

We put up a tent as soon as I had realised this had happened which admittedly was some time in the future. I made the cups of hot chocolate but instead of cooking the supper I put my hand in a flask of hot water to try and ensure that any coldness still in my hand was removed. Having defrosted the hands I then put my hand under Alex's armpit as this and the groin is the warmest place on your body. Later, I moved and held my hands on my groin within my sleeping bag. With hindsight I would have done this straight away rather than waste Alex's time. Within this time, Alex cooked supper for us all which was not really his job but I was very grateful for his help. When we managed to call the camp we had to tell them about Alex being up again and me being injured. I spoke to the base camp and they seemed more than happy with me being able to continue.

The next day we were able to start again and for the first time in three days we would actually have a full day out on the ice but by now we really had no chance of winning the race. We got moving and just kept going as far as we could. That evening we rang in, as per usual, but received some frightening news. Alex was doing the call and because we were still on the ice we could not hear too much of it but Alex soon brought us up to speed with what had happened.

Alex came off the phone and told us that the Channel Islanders had had to shoot a polar bear because they had been asleep and were woken up by a bear knocking on the tent. This was my worst nightmare to come so close to a bear that you actually had to shoot at it. I was quite surprised by the amount of information Alex had been able to gather in a short call but obviously the organisers wanted us to know and be aware that it may happen again.

Apparently when they shot the bear and rang in to declare it, they were asked if they had shot a male or a female. Obviously they didn't know so asked if there was any way they could tell, and got asked how big it was. They said it's about five foot to which the authorities said "it is probably a female so you don't have to worry, but it could be an adolescent male in which case its parents will be looking for him, so you probably would want to get about five miles from there as soon as possible". Not surprisingly, they assumed the worst and moved as quickly as they could from the area. I say as quickly as they could because it took time to pack everything up and move at the North Pole.

It turned out it was a female so they needn't have panicked but, better safe than sorry, particularly with polar bears. As this happened in a race, there became a situation with the time it took them. A bear is not really a race issue so it was quite right that they had a small deduction of time and I think they did. I was considering we complained about this as even I would have got up quickly and moved away from the site very speedily so I thought they should actually be docked time. We thought about it but obviously did nothing.

The following day Charlie was the third of us being ill. We awoke as normal, but this time Charlie said he was ill and couldn't move to start with. We obviously agreed and I continued doing what I normally did and we allowed Charlie some time. Four hours or so he awoke and Alex and I thought he would say goodnight and pack up for the day but he was incredible. He just said we ought to think about going but were a bit late today. He sounded brilliant, I don't know what it was but he had just slept it off. We eventually got going and because of Charlie's attitude we all had a good attitude that day. By now we had lost so much time that we were no longer worried about the race and it was now just about reaching the pole. We came to a boulder field which is a section of the sea ice that has frozen badly and it leaves a huge amount of funny ice shapes in the ground. Obviously these boulder fields are best ignored, but if you cannot see a way around them you just have to be careful and go through. So we headed into the boulder field and were amazed at how big it was. It just kept going and going. It was now approaching the time to camp up for the day and still it went on. At a break, we had a quick discussion about this but the only option was to keep going until we were through the field.

We were due to fire a few bullets every now and then to ensure the guns were working satisfactorily, maybe one to two every ten days or so. We discovered another team had gone through the field as well and decided it would be a good idea to test their gun, only they tested it several times against the same boulder. It was now past the normal time that we would set up camp. I knew the score, we had to get out of the boulder field as, although it was unlikely that polar bears would be around, we couldn't see them coming and that was just asking for trouble. Even so, I was getting frustrated as I wanted to have a decent meal and go to sleep. Just as suddenly as it first appeared it disappeared and we thought we were through it.

Everyone knows the joke about not drinking yellow snow but we weren't worried about that. We were worried about blue snow because blue snow occurs just above the water as it is the salt in the water. If this does occur, it is likely to be near the edge of a boulder field. So, before we set up camp we thought we should check vigorously that the snow wasn't blue. It clearly wasn't and now I don't really know why we went to such effort.

We eventually camped up and got ourselves ready for the next day when hopefully we would reach checkpoint two. It had been a long and bad journey but tomorrow the weather was looking clear and we were near the checkpoint. The next day came and we were very optimistic as we set off knowing we should reach camp. The day was fantastic and we steadily approached the camp.

We were getting very near the camp but we couldn't see it. We stopped and checked the location and agreed where it ought to be, but it wasn't. We decided that they must be over the hill so we began walking to get up and over the hill. As we got about halfway up the hill, someone actually spotted the camp and it was where they said it should be. I don't know how, but somehow we had managed to walk straight past it probably within half a mile or so. The camp organizers had seen us going past and had sent out a couple of people to come and get us although we had, by then, seen where we should be. We headed for the camp in a very jovial mood as now we had done the worst leg and it would get better from now on although I had to pass the doctor's visit we assumed he would just tell me to be careful in the future.

At camp, the first thing we did was sit down for a cup of coffee. Alex got the race scores which confirmed we didn't need to worry about the race anymore but I just settled down for a nice cup of coffee made by someone else. It was the doctor's job to check up on us all at the checkpoint and, given that Alex had rung in on my behalf with frostbite, he soon made his way to me to begin a check-up. Alex and Charlie were watching this but no one believed there would be anything wrong. Alex joked to the doctor "is that it for David then?" at which point the doctor, in all seriousness, said "yes". I was distraught and I think the other two were upset although no one said a word our faces had all changed. The doctor looked at us and realised what he had said and responded "sorry, David is fine, I thought you meant the guy from the other team". We were all and I, particularly, so were relieved.

The person who had unfortunately got frostbite on the first leg quite badly which had refrozen could not continue out on the ice. He would stay at the basecamp under the supervision of the doctor until we left and he would then fly back and get whatever medical treatment he could. This was sad for us to lose a race member but fortunately he was from the four-person team so at least they could all still make it there. I don't know exactly what he had done bit he was responsible for holding the gun throughout the trip and one day he announced when they had stopped for a break that he didn't have the gun and they needed to travel back for a distance of no one really knows. This would have been bad enough on a normal day but this was a particularly bad day of weather and they had to follow their tracks backwards. I don't what I would have said but I wouldn't have been keen to go backwards and I assume they would have been the same. I had to say, I was glad it wasn't our team.

Some other race members who had been there quite a while said they would put up the tent while we rested a bit and had our coffee. We were ecstatic to let them do this and we stayed in the main tent and let them put it up. As we were staying, I decided to take off my face mask as I did so the race leader decided to help. In so doing he tore the mask off not realizing it was still attached to my nose. It felt like he had ripped my nose off although, in actual fact, it was only a small wound. It made me realise how much more used to these sorts of climates he was as he had no idea what he had done and, even less, that I might be bothered. The race leader was one of the politest people you could ever meet but he had no consideration for the fact that I might be even the tiniest bit upset.

As we had taken so long on the second leg we only had a short time at the camp but at least we had a couple of nights before we had to go again. There were the normal routine jobs with checking the new supplies but these were relatively few and there was plenty of time for them.

Although I probably could have coped with another day it was fine to leave when we did.

6   Leg 3

Leg three would start at two o'clock in the afternoon, but for some reason the race leader had decided we would have a meeting beforehand. I had no interest in this as my sole concern was finishing the race but as he wanted a meeting we would go. The meeting was alright, but I just wanted to leave and as soon as it finished, I was gone. From then on in, we got ready for the race. The next leg was approximately ninety miles but the weather had improved dramatically and I was optimistic for this leg. We now knew we had no chance of winning the race and we probably would be fourth so we could now travel as per how we wanted.

I don't know how it happened but, as we were swapping our bags for the next leg with the race organisers, somehow my photo card went missing and I lost all my photographs of the second leg. This was extremely disappointing at the time but the truth is there weren't that many and I got everyone else's photographs at the end so it didn't really matter.

The third leg was ready to go and, to this day, I don't know what happened but when the organiser said "go" and fired his gun, I walked a couple of steps and realised my sled was not attached to me! Everyone else was racing and moving forward as per usual but I was still to get going. I ran back to the start and grabbed the sled but the man who was out of the race stopped me and connected me to the sled. We lost a couple of minutes but I was, in fact I still am, embarrassed about that. We soon regained the time lost at the start and we did have a story for that night. Throughout the leg we were racing two teams with one team behind us and the South Africans still a day behind, but we were totally unable to see the two doctors. My suspicions were that they had gone ahead and now realised they could spend time on the ice and they would go on and win the leg. Unfortunately they had spent a lot of time on the second leg playing around so it was unlikely they would win although they were probably the fastest.

We were moving reasonably well on this leg and I thought I was nicely settled in with the cooking, however, one night I had decided I would make a strong cup of hot chocolate for everyone but Charlie said I had made it too weak. I was incensed how it could be too weak when I had put an extra amount in. This was probably the only argument we had the entire trip and it went on for about fifteen minutes with me saying I put more in and him saying he couldn't understand what I did when we stopped. It stopped because Alex who had been butting in and out suddenly said "did you change from British to Canadian chocolate today?" He was totally correct, it hadn't even crossed my mind but obviously the British chocolate was stronger. I immediately apologised to everyone there, particularly Charlie. They very graciously accepted the apology and we agreed that now we only had the Canadian chocolate I would use a lot more and, if we ran out, then we would go back to coffee. We slept that night a little bit apprehensive after what was said but one argument in a trip like that is pretty good.

We set off the next day knowing the two teams we were racing had already gone past us but we weren't really bothered with the race and we knew we would go on longer anyway. It was quite nice having the other people go past our tent whilst we were cooking and having a brief chat with them.

During this leg we had now got familiar with storing our equipment and now fully understood any area within the tent is usable and if you need a space and some area is free just use it. This was particularly apparent to space off the ground. The row of four bits of rope holding our tent in shape was now a mass of items and now looked more like a great big washing line than a piece of tent. I decided I would take some photographs of this. I am not really sure why but the photograph of me next to the enormous washing line is one I hold very dear to me. I am told I look ill in it, and I probably do but that is how I felt so I am not that worried about it.

The third leg was going very well but two things made me realise just how much better Alex and Charlie were doing than I was. The first was when Alex mentioned to Charlie that they will soon be at the pole and wasn't it fantastic now we were at that point to which Charlie immediately replied "oh yes" but when they asked me I had to respond I said "I am not at that point yet and probably won't be until we are two or three miles away at most". I was encouraged by the response though. They said "you've got this far with us, we will tow you and our sleds to get you to finish". I don't know how serious they were that they would try to find a way to the pole but it cheered me up anyway. The second factor was Alex was starting to decide on which wine he would have when he finished and he was trying to organise a party for the group in our Ottawa hotel when we finished. He used the daily phone call to the base camp to set out a full wine order. I found the enthusiasm and comfort he showed in doing this on stage three quite extraordinary.

The last day on this leg the sun was wonderful. It was about minus five as opposed to typically minus twenty five and perhaps minus forty, but the sun was out. Even I wore slightly less than usual but Alex actually went topless which makes perfect sense if you were there but on the face of it sounds like madness. Alex was using a lot of energy each day and had sun directly on him so it would have felt warm. Like I said I felt warm but not that warm.

Throughout the last day we kept meeting up with the teams we were racing against as we were all in much the same position but, because we awoke at different times, we stopped for breaks at different stages. If you stopped someone would catch up with you. We began talking about whether we would go through the night or not. We reckoned if we gave up at the normal time we would have around fourteen miles to go which would take around seven hours the next day. The other two had told us they weren't going to bother but we had said we hadn't decided yet. The reality was it would come down to me. Alex and Charlie would keep going until we got there but I didn't know how I would feel. The beautiful weather was meaning I was keen to go but I wanted to have supper first to which the others agreed and, as long as the weather stayed warm, we would then move on.

We decided to stop and set up a sort of half camp. We got the tent up but didn't worry about snow to partially bury it and we took out the cooking stuff and the sleeping bags to keep us warm but nothing else. I cooked as quickly as I could and then we were ready to go again. Had I had a truly free vote I probably would have stayed and got to camp later the next day but it was clear from looking at Alex and Charlie that I would have to have a good reason. We went the first day knowing there was a chance we could win the leg but in reality the two doctors were already there.

We set off and I was so pleased we did. That night of travelling it got a bit colder but was not at all unpleasant and so that night became my personal highlight of the entire trip. We had been travelling some time and were going to have a stop for some food when we realised it was nearly midnight. We decided we would make sure we were stopped at that point because although we hated taking photographs the scenery was incredible and the midnight air was fantastic. We knew the sun had gone down and it was definitely night time but you could still see everything. We stopped and I took two photographs of Charlie from behind. I don't have many pictures out at home but that is one which I have increased to full page size and keep on my wall. The other one I keep at home is the three of us as we finished the trip.

We carried on and eventually got in at about four in the morning. No one was awake so we took a photograph of our time and a copy of the GPS reading so they would know exactly how long it had taken. As we had expected, the two doctors were tucked up nicely in their tent but we weren't really worried about the race as we were so far behind. The real beauty is that we would get up when we felt like it and effectively had an extra day at the checkpoint.

As part of the camp they had made a small igloo. Whilst I thought it was interesting that someone had done that it is as far as my thoughts went. Alex wanted to try everything out and so he arranged to sleep in it the first night which made me think "great, a bit more room in the tent!" He slept in it and apparently it was very comfortable but I was far happier knowing where everything was. It did make me realise how bored the race organisers got when they set up base camp. They didn't really have anything to do. Firstly, they were there before us and they left after us so they were at the base camp for a reasonably long time. Secondly, they were not tired and exhausted when they arrived and, thirdly, they didn't have any chores to do. It must actually have been very boring for the two or three who arrived at the checkpoints. My original thought of the putting up the igloo to be creative and artistic was actually rubbish. They did it for something to do.

We were quite happy for a couple of days but we fully understood the final leg was coming and this was a short leg. The day arrived where we would start our final leg. It was approximately fifty miles and we thought, at a push, we can do it in two days. The two doctors were on about doing it continually but they still had a chance of winning. The male and female team were winning comfortably but would go continuously as well, but we were so far back it didn't matter. What mattered was getting to the North Pole.

7   Leg 4

Still we had all the final days' duties to get through first and, yet again, the organisers had booked a special meeting for us. Again we went to the meeting, but didn't really want to. I suspect this was caused by the meeting as we only found out about it later on but somehow we missed the timing of this and although we got to the meeting alright, it put us behind with packing up. The meeting was similar to the last leg it was great to be well wished away but, at that point in time, I would have preferred to just have been kicked off and left to travel as it suited us.

Anyway, we were now free to start moving and, for some reason, we were slow at packing up that day. When they came to restart the race we were still a few minutes from ready. We asked if the rest of them could go as we would catch them up but the organisers said no. It didn't really bother us but keeping the others waiting for about fifteen minutes probably annoyed them to no end.

Once we were off again, the two doctors went their own way and it was clear they would finish before us but we stayed with the two other two man teams and walked with them on the first night. Whilst walking with the male and female team it was quite amusing because everyone else knew that they had swapped the tent topping with the Channel Islanders. The Channel Islanders had shot a hole in theirs so they had received a new topping at the second checkpoint. They had only managed a red one whereas everyone else had the original green. I don't really know why they did it as they reached the pole without stopping but just keeping the subterfuge going was fun.

We decided to stop at the same time as the Channel Islanders but the male and female team were going to win and so had to keep going. As we stopped, we decided to make our daily report to base camp. The Channel Islanders rang and then transferred the phone to Alex to talk. They accepted the call but you could tell they were slightly irritated that we had walked together but the race was over for both of our teams.

The Channel Islanders got up first and left us behind the next morning. This would normally have been a bad thing but the weather had other ideas. They went off about two hours ahead of us. We could tell the weather was not too good but tucked up in the tent it is difficult to say just how bad. It was a very short storm but it was horrid. As they were out in the full force of it they decided they would have to camp up and stay in the tent until it was over. This meant the three of us were able to see them camping and overtake them on the leg. The problem with setting up camp was, it took such a long time to get going again.

We kept going and to do this in two shifts was going to be difficult and I genuinely wished we had decided to take three shifts, particularly as the weather, whilst allowing us out was doing its best to slow us down. Anyway we had had the discussion and it was going to be done in two shifts and I had accepted this. The other two were significantly better than me and I had slowed them down enough already and this was the last leg so I would just take it. Having said all of that, with hindsight it was totally the right thing to do.

I was struggling a bit and this was obvious to the others. We were getting near the end of the trip and we came to a small hill probably about fifteen feet high. Before we climbed it, we were having a break and Alex said the pole is quite near. We could either climb the hill or walk around it. Much to everyone's amazement, I responded with "do we think there are hills behind because there is no problem climbing those, but if there are others?" We looked at the map and couldn't see any more so we went for it.

Amazingly we were correct, it was just over the hills there were no other hills and then it was a simple walk to the pole. We had discussed how we would reach the pole in terms of the order we would be in but as we got there the order was obvious. There could be no order we had set off as a team and we would arrive together as a team. I knew Alex and Charlie had helped me get there but that was because I was in their team and I don't know about them but it was definitely right for me.

We had a photograph taken off us as we reached the North Pole where the three of us our hugging each other with gratitude for arriving. This is the other photograph I have had enlarged and keep out, even though I have disappeared in the photograph and only my head and hands are showing, but I know what the photograph means.

8   Celebrating the North Pole

When we had arrived at the North Pole, I was able to celebrate, but it was still cold and I was not as into it as much as the other people. The first day we arrived, I was elated, but it was late so I spent a few minutes in the main tent with the race organisers and they had brought the man who dropped out of the race after leg two. Personally, I was quite pleased to see him because, although he could be quite annoying, he had paid a lot of money to get there. I am not sure how the other competitors felt.

The next morning I went to make hot chocolate drinks as usual and I had two surprises. Firstly, there was a new tent and I knew it was not from our race. Normally I wouldn't worry about it at all but at the North Pole it didn't seem right. Secondly, I went to clear the left overs out from last night and for the first time they were not frozen. They were very slushy but not actually frozen so this meant the temperature was low by UK standards but quite high for the North Pole at, give or take, freezing.

Soon after we had finished our breakfast, one of the race organisers appeared at the tent and said he had been chatting at the new tent. It was the first group of racers from the other race which considering they were about a week behind us was impressive. He then asked if we had any coffee left as they had run out and would like pure coffee again. We duly handed over a small carton of coffee and he presented us with some sachets they had given him but we didn't really want them.

It was quite strange as we had at least a day at the pole with absolutely nothing to do. This was the first time for ages I had nothing to do. We knew it would be at least a day as all the race organisers had been on the phone to the airline and they were all helping some Korean team out. It made you realise it was hugely efficient, but there are only a couple of planes still doing this. I did make the effort to go outside twice but it was still cold and I didn't need to that often although I heard one of the Channel Islanders had some sloe gin so I went out then and one other time when I was being bayed at to appear. The rest of the time I remained in my tent, happy that I had finished my trip and ironically now wishing to return. I say ironically because the two doctors who had arrived before the race organisers were given the choice of returning to Resolute Bay with the plane, or staying and waiting for us. They chose to return with the plane. It does make you realise this was very much about the trip and not the destination.

The next day when we knew the plane was coming for us it was about getting packed up and waiting for the plane. I was quite happy about this; we had got all the photographs of the North Pole together with various flags and badges.

I hadn't really thought about it but I awoke every ninety minutes on the ice presumably because I was scared of the cold but once I got on the plane back I went to sleep. I remember waking once to see the South African team who were still trekking towards the pole. It is amazing what the visibility can be like there because obviously the pilot had seen them some way away and was flying down a lot lower than normal so we could see them, and just as impressive was that they had seen us.

We got back to Resolute Bay and we were just another group of people but we all felt different. The first thing we did back at the base was get weighed and give the kit back to Jock. At the weigh in it was quite revealing in that the other people in the race had lost around one kilogram whereas I was just less than one pound. This is a significant difference but one I have always been used to. I was not surprised although others were. Handing back the kit took about five minutes because we just wanted it done and then we could enjoy the area and more importantly reaching the North Pole.

The most important thing for all of us to do was to have a shower. We had spent three weeks on the ice often not changing clothes and that was how it was when you were trekking so it was time to have a shower. I was conscious the other two needed a shower as well so I made sure I was clean and I mean clean and then struggled to clean the shower before leaving it to Alex. As Alex went into the shower it became clear that Charlie had done it deliberately because he had something to tell me. I was aware that he had something wrong with his stomach because this had happened on leg one. He went to the toilet and put his sled on but left it dragging against his stomach rather than pulling in his shoulders via the harness. He ignored this then but afterwards had to have skin grafts to help it heal properly.

The second thing he wanted to tell us shocked me more, not because it had happened, but because neither I nor Alex realised. He took off his inner layer of gloves and I realised that he too had got frostbite on his hands and again this happened on the first leg. The fact that he had kept it secret for so long in a small tent like that was a testament to his determination and his bravery, but equally, fairly irritating.

Resolute Bay has a bit more going for it than the pole as a venue to go to but I wouldn't recommend either of them as a holiday venue. As for celebrating the North Pole, it was difficult here as Resolute Bay was a dry town in that all alcohol was banned. Admittedly we did get a bottle of champagne inside our bedroom but we could hardly shout about it, still we only had one night here and I was tired.

As Jock put it; Resolute Bay is a dry town because the Inuit's find alcohol very strong and it doesn't go with their DNA so they would have a drink and then ride their snowmobiles until they fell off. After they had picked so many frozen Inuit's out of the snow they decided to make alcohol illegal. We obviously needed to be aware of this; hence we were very private with our alcohol.

I had to ring my parents just to let them know I was back, alive and permanently undamaged. I only had time for a brief conversation with them but it was enough. I found out how difficult my mother had found the trip but equally how impressed she was that I had managed it. I arranged for them to go to Winchester where I lived on the following Saturday.

The next day we got to fly back to Ottawa. We were only there a couple of days but it was magical for me. It was the first time for around eighteen months where I would be somewhere and not be thinking of getting to the North Pole and I was determined to enjoy it. I am not sure if Ottawa was a very exciting place or not, I suspect not, but for me it was extraordinary. We went into Ottawa pretty much as a group, but that was fine, we were a group at that point and I think we all wanted to tell the world what we had done.

Walking into the town one racer turned to me and said I am so glad you can walk properly, which made me smile but then I thought about it. He, like me, was relieved to be walking with someone whose actual pace was akin to their own. This was in fact a relief, as prior to walking to the pole, I had been getting faster and faster and when walking with my friends I had become conscious if needing to slow down, whereas with him I was at my own pace.

I was in Ottawa for the day but I didn't feel the need to move that far. It was fantastic sitting in a bar and just looking at what Ottawa had to offer. I went for a brief shopping trip because to have bought nothing would just be wrong but there was no rhyme or reason to what I would get apart from a small cuddly polar bear to remind me I had walked to the North Pole.

That evening we were going out for dinner but, beforehand, Alex was holding his party. We were all going to go which was excellent and sums up the camaraderie we had even if we were racing each other. I got ready for the party but, more explicitly, I got ready to go out afterwards. The party was a bit too early but the wine was fantastic and we had the whole group together which was lovely at the end of the race and the last time we were all together. I don't remember much about the dinner although I did have a long chat to the South African team. They wanted to have my photograph for when they did the presentation of the trip to other people as they felt that, while no one was particularly like Scott, I was the least like him of anyone. Later on I discovered if they were ever down in their tent they would say you could be David. David is in another tent and making the most of it so you must be able to as well.

97

We were returning to the UK and I heard Tony Blair had been re-elected as prime minister. The real joy of this was that I had completely missed his election campaign. He had announced it the day I left for the North Pole and got re-elected the day before I was returning. The result where I lived was as expected and my vote was unnecessary because that was the first and only general election I have not voted at.

We arrived home and, before we could say goodbye, we had to split our goodies up. Most of this had already been done but I needed my skis and poles, although we could only find one ski. This was a bit disappointing but I was never going to use them again so it didn't really matter. I also needed my sled which again I didn't know what I would do with it but that didn't really matter either. Charlie had got all the sleds together for our team and just took out a knife and cut them apart, unfortunately this meant he cut the strapping off my sled, but again, it didn't matter.

Then we went through customs and re-joined our normal lives. I noticed Charlie was a bit ahead of me and his wife recognised him but his young child did not because he had a huge beard he had grown over the past three or four weeks. I then met up with my girlfriend and she was due to take me home, although my parents were coming in the afternoon. Seeing my parents was fantastic as they were incredibly happy with what I had done.

The next day was a Sunday so I had one day at home before going back to work and trying to catch up on anything that had arisen in the past five weeks. Unfortunately, I had taken almost the entire year's holiday in one hit so it would be back to work for a long time once I returned.

I got up and went to work. It was quite amusing, I was ready to work but equally I was quite happy just talking about the North Pole. I arrived at about eight o'clock as usual and generally waited for people to come in. One disappointment was the marketing girl we had who had put so much into my trip from a marketing viewpoint, but had handed her notice in as I left and had done her one month's notice before I returned. Unfortunately, despite setting everything up she was unable to see it through which was a big shame but she obviously thought her career was bigger than my trip, at least for her.

During my read through of e-mails I had missed throughout the five weeks was one sent by the marketing girl to the entire office containing news about my team winning the first leg and it became apparent that the office had been reading the polar race website every day to see how things were getting on. I don't really know why I was surprised because, if someone I knew was in the race, I would follow it as well but it did give me a sense of pride. It was also apparent that my completion of this task had gone around the firm and this also made me proud because never had someone's break time been the subject of such widespread interest from around the firm. In fact, going through my e-mails brought me a great sense of pride because, although work e-mails got in the way, the majority of them were individual messages of applause from anyone I knew. I got a message from my friend in Australia again making it clear he had kept in touch with the race on the website. Perhaps the message that gave me the most satisfaction was from a friend of mine but the thing that was so amazing was that he had half a page of type basically saying how well he had thought I had done. A fellow Tabler sent an e-mail simply saying 'bloody well done' which was far simpler but just as well appreciated.

As I had now returned, Baker Tilly felt it was best to get some last minute marketing in and arranged for me to have a local radio station and a couple of local papers interview me now that I had actually done it. After this, I had one last thing to do at Baker Tilly, which was a marketing interview saying that I had reached the North Pole and what I thought of it. There were about forty clients there which was fantastic.

The celebration party had been flagged by Jock a long way off, in fact before we actually went to the Arctic, but I had never really embraced the concept probably because I didn't want to think about a celebration when I still had the pole to reach. However, once I returned home, I was fairly excited about it all. I arrived at the event which was to be headed by the official leader of the event, but we were met by a slightly furtive Jock who said the official leader was going to do a pre-dinner speech as he had to get home. It wasn't until later that night that we knew why. There was apparently some press coverage of him and a lady friend coming out over the weekend and he needed to be with his wife!

There was another speaker but that wasn't what this event was about. It was about seeing everyone else again and just remembering how good a trip it actually was. The party went on and, in fact, it literally went on all night. Although I had booked a hotel I didn't sleep a single second in the bed. We finished having breakfast in the Ritz Hotel. The thing that amazed me about this is that everyone got on so well with each other and fully respected everyone for making it to the pole no matter how they managed. It was just a shame the South Africans couldn't make it.

I was going to give a number of speeches about this to various organisations in and around Winchester, but the first people to get me to one of their meetings was Winchester Ladies' Circle. I am still impressed by how long I went on for and, more impressively, was their keenness for me to do so. They said "just keep speaking and we will stop you when we are ready". I probably started about nine o'clock but carried on until mid-night.

The last people I had to tell about getting to the pole were the Round Tablers. First, I needed to tell Winchester Round Table and they had booked a few minutes to talk about it at one of their meetings. Unfortunately, there were several speakers that night and they took the limelight a bit, but I knew I would see and tell them again. I had a Winchester rosette at the pole and I had a photograph taken with it and got it stamped with a polar bear picture. I set these up in a clear glass frame but, alas, the waiter went and trod on it before I could give it to the Chairman. I still gave it, but it was not the same with all the glass removed.

As far as the European Tables were concerned, this year, by good fortune, we were in Finland. As the Finns had helped me get ready for the pole, I felt it only proper to arrange a gift for them. They too had given me a Finnish rosette so I did the same as for Winchester but their waiters were better and it was still whole when it came to give it to them. It is a Table tradition you should try and steal the gifts for a year. So you take it one year knowing you will return the next year. I don't know why but I thought my gift should not be taken but it was. The Germans returned it to the Finns the next year.

9   Back home

I didn't realise it at the time but the fact is that one of the reasons for going to the North Pole was that I knew I had to leave Baker Tilly but didn't know the best way to do it, but now I was back from the Pole I could live off that for a bit, but eventually I needed to leave. At first, I was able to get back into the swing of Baker Tilly but long term it was different.

When I was first back at work, it was much like the old story only I was now talking to everyone about going to the North Pole and this would do for a good year. One of the big problems I had was, apart from the celebration party and the trip to Finland with Round Table accounting for three days leave, I had no more holidays until the next April. This wasn't actually that bad, but knowing you couldn't take leave made you want it even more.

The first couple of months back at work I was extremely mentally fit and ready. This surprised me because I had expected that, because I was physically tired, I would be mentally as well, but in fact I had had five weeks not worrying about accounting issues so when I went back to work I was incredibly refreshed and invigorated. This was a major surprise to me and incredibly welcome because I knew I had a bit of catching up to do at work and this gave me the bit of a push I needed. In the summer, an old friend of mine decided that he would hold a barbecue and invited me. I don't think it was deliberate but he made me feel like a guest of honour regarding the North Pole. His brother insisted on shaking my hand because he wanted to shake the hand of a polar visitor. He had some other friends who he wanted me to talk to but the most interesting was Jacki. I was still seeing someone else at the time although before I went that night, I knew that was going to be short lived. Having met Jacki I knew I would end up with her but at this stage I had no idea how or when it was going to happen.

It would be a good few months before I had the courage to get in touch with Jacki but Round Table were holding a dinner and dance the following first of April and my friend and his wife were coming as my guest so I made them ask Jacki as well so that we would go as a foursome. Unbeknown to the three of us the week before the dinner Jacki had decided to go to New York and so we didn't get a reply. Jacki saying no would have been disappointing but acceptable but Jacki not replying was just plain rude. Anyway, Jacki did return from New York well in time to be my guest and I was highly delighted she said yes. I spoke to her and she agreed she would see me afterwards as well.

About three months or so before this event I had booked a holiday to the Galapagos Islands also stopping at Ecuador and Peru. I had booked this trip when I was alone and, as such, booked it for one. Jacki was very good about this, although I did promise that subsequent trips would be for two people, but this was just for one. By completing this trip I would have done six continents and a pole. The only continent needed to complete the traveller's grand slam.

The holiday was in September 2006 and at the time I was sure it was just one of many holidays so, although I was now seeing Jacki and intended to continue seeing her, I was not afraid to go. Before I went I thought it would be good to book her a bunch of flowers to be delivered exactly half way through the holiday and, by an act of chance, it coincided with the date that a former ex of hers was going to visit her at home.

The holiday began and I met up with the group of people who would also be on the trip with me. The first day began with an older woman who had left her mobile telephone in the hold of the aeroplane and she needed to get the battery recharged but she hadn't brought the charger. We should have known then that she was a stupid woman but that was quite a mild event.

The trip was effectively a wildlife visit but there were also a few cultural visits. The first part of the trip was to stay at a nature reserve just off a subsidiary off the Amazon and was fantastic. We went on a general tour of the reserve during the day which was excellent, but the tour guide said we could also be taken after dark if we chose to. There were four single males, of which I was one, on the trip and we decided we would go on a night time trip which was remarkable. There were scary points during the day trip as there were certain dangerous animals, but during the night when you cannot see what is there, it was truly frightening. We then discovered that the next night no one else wanted to go so the organiser agreed to take the four of us again.

The next trip was to the 'top of the Amazon'. We went to the heart of the Amazon forest and then got taken up the highest tree so we were able to look down on all the other trees and the Amazon as a whole. When we went back to the camp site it became apparent that the older woman had a habit of saying things before thinking about them and one of the other single males was very good at teasing her about her comments. The first I became aware of this talent was with a cricket we saw at the camp site. He asked what it ate to become the florescent colour that it was and he then immediately followed it with the answer that it was the mobile phone battery! Having made this comment he then followed it up throughout the holiday as a whole. I suppose, in thinking about it, we were quite rude about her but she said and did several things that didn't make sense. At one stage on this trip we were in a low levelled boat and the water level had risen overnight dramatically. She put her hand on the water which in itself was brave but then she licked it dry.

On one day we tried fishing for piranhas. This was actually quite difficult because it was impossible to see into the water as the water was itself so dirty. I personally failed in my attempt to catch a piranha but a couple of piranhas were caught and we were able to see just how powerful their mouths were. It still seems strange to have gone fishing with lumps of meat as the bait.

The next day we are at the Machu Picchu and there was a chance to climb the mountain. The trip organiser was so fearful of this climb that she almost put me off because she kept warning of the dangers of climbing it and threatening us about exhaustion and a lack of water. Eventually there were enough members of the group intent on climbing it so I decided to as well. It was relatively easy, if taken sensibly and slowly. We arrived at Machu Picchu already most of the way up and we only went about three or four hundred metres up and it was well monitored and maintained. We had a brief stay at the top and I fully understand why so many people do the Inca Trail because the views from the top were amazing.

That evening we went around the small town and did a bit of shopping. I felt guilty about not being with Jacki and I bought her an alpaca jumper which I gave her on my return. She loved it, but unfortunately she wore it once and then washed it in a washing machine and it shrunk and doesn't fit any more. It was a bit disappointing, but our baggage allowance for the flight to the Galapagos Islands was a bit lower than the main flight back and this restricted some of the purchases we could make. Then we actually got to the flight it appeared they had amended this and so we could have made the extra purchases but I haven't missed any purchases so I guess it doesn't matter. The best bit about the flight to Galapagos Islands was the approach in. The runway was incredibly near to the coast so the approach in felt like you were landing on the sea.

Having arrived there, we queued up for a while to pay the duty of staying in the Galapagos Islands which was a reasonable cost but, apparently, it was to continue their funding of wildlife-related issues, so I personally didn't object. What I hadn't realised about the islands and, it seems silly given their name, but I hadn't really understood that everywhere was a unique island and had its own wildlife base. As a result of this our trip was a cruise around some of the islands.

The islands were visited very much according to a schedule that had clearly been agreed with the island authorities in advance. They didn't draw attention to it but it was clear that we were given a specific number of minutes for each area and the tour guide was required to find things to do or talk about if we were running ahead and to cut things if we were running behind. Whilst we were doing the tour we got to see Lonesome George, the sole surviving tortoise of his particular species who, to a large extent, was responsible for the current success of the islands and unfortunately he has since died. The other thing I saw that was new to me was a small flock of penguins. These particular penguins were on one island and are the only penguins who reside in the northern hemisphere. The two things that were pretty much on any island were the equatorial iguanas and the large amount of seals. Throughout the course of this trip I realised that the islands were all remarkably small. There were a couple of bigger islands which had people living on them but most of them we would go on and we would walk around the island in a few hours. The older woman came up with some classic statements during this trip including describing lizards as four-eyed when the additional two were simply eye lashes!

The Galapagos Islands were undoubtedly the highlight of the trip for me but this section had now finished and we were going to Ecuador for a couple of days before returning home. We arrived in Ecuador and spent the day in Quito which I knew was the world's highest capital city, but it was not until I stayed there that I fully appreciated how high it was. We did a final bit of shopping but the reality was that the trip was more or less over and we knew it, so we shopped a bit but mainly relaxed.

I had realised Jacki was the right woman for me long ago so in November I decided to do something about it and I proposed. To my relief she said yes and we would get married the next year. This may appear a bit dramatic, but it certainly didn't feel that way. We both knew what we wanted and getting married was the easiest way of doing it. No one, except our Tax Partner, really knew about Jacki so they weren't expecting an announcement so soon but that just made it better. I decided I would take in some champagne and announce it formally which I think was well received.

Christmas came and we had decided to spend it in South Africa and visit Jacki's step mother in Johannesburg and friends down in Port Elizabeth before going to Cape Town. This would be my first experience of South Africa so I was very excited about it and Jacki new the place so she was going to go to all the right places. Before we left it had got off to a very promising start with Phinda Game Reserve. Jacki had booked us in for a few nights at the game reserve and booked from England, paying for it by credit card. For some reason they took the payment twice. Jacki asked them to clear it which they did but it didn't quite refund the amount she had overpaid because the exchange rate had lessoned so Jacki asked them again and this time they said "come for free" and refunded Jacki's entire payment! I didn't know anything about Phinda but I knew about staying on a game reserve so I was very excited about this even if it was only for a few days.

We arrived at Johannesburg airport and we were met by Jacki's step mother. I then got my first real memory of South Africa. As we were leaving the airport her step mother put the ticket into the machine but then stopped. Jacki had told me that you don't stop at traffic lights if there is nothing coming for fear of being car jacked so I had expected her to go quickly from the airport. She was actually waiting because she knew, but I hadn't seen, in addition to the bar at eye level they had also got controls in at ground level. Two sets of blades had come up above the ground and were very slow in going back below ground level and quite correctly, she was waiting for them to return to the ground and be certain they had returned before we left the airport.

The time in Johannesburg was interesting and worthwhile but I feel this is more to do with us knowing someone. We had a great time there, but I suspect there is little we would have been able to do if we had arrived there unknown to the locals, but knowing people certainly made it fun and the weather in December was fantastic, although somewhat difficult to live with given the altitude. The altitude, on two occasions made my nose bleed, and we suffered from thunder storms given the temperature but that was nothing really. The good thing about the weather was that once the storm had finished it was nicely cooled down and you could easily go outside again.

After a couple of days in Johannesburg I was quite happy to leave it and fly to Phinda. I had been looking forward to this, but knowing it was free somehow made it more special. I don't know why, but I hadn't realised how few people went there and so at Johannesburg airport we couldn't find anyone who knew about it even though we were where the tickets said we should be, but we were early. At exactly the time they said a couple of people arrived checked our tickets and then agreed to take us and one other person. We then got walked for what seemed like miles to a small runway and then boarded the aeroplane. The couple that met us became responsible for flying the machine and it would sit another four or five at a push, but very comfortably.

Arriving at Phinda, we got shown to our glass cabin. Actually, it was a standalone glass box with plenty of room and a fantastic all round view. We didn't know but, apparently it was on a sand forest, very famous as the only sand forest in the world. I don't really know what difference this made but one thing was certain Phinda was an excellent place to spend a few days of unadulterated self-indulgence along with the chance of two very long game drives a day. I am not sure how I feel about the content of the game drives because it came clear that they only had a few of the big five and they were tagged so they could find them easily. I suppose it made sense, and we did see them all, but it somehow felt like cheating.

Phinda was great for us as we both have a great liking of wildlife and it was totally relaxing which was something I had missed from a holiday since I went to Kenya. Unfortunately, it was over all too soon but we did have a chance to purchase a few things from there shop. It took a few minutes to choose them but then it took ages not to agree the discount of fifteen percent but to explain how it worked. The amount involved meant the shop assistant needed to enter it on the cash point machine twice for some reason. She decided she would give ten percent to the large amount and five percent to the balance. I explained the percentage must be deducted in full from both amounts and it took a few hours for her to agree with me. Even now, I am not sure whether she agreed or just felt it was worth listening to in order to get a sale, but eventually she agreed.

We were due to leave Phinda the next day but before we went they provided an open air meal for us most of which was cooked on a braai, meaning the meat in particular was superb. The game drives we had had were together with one other couple who were from America and on honeymoon. This outdoor meal was the first time we knew they were on honeymoon and they thought they had trumped us with that but we had not told them about the North Pole. I have now been in South Africa a lot and for some reason almost everyone is truly appreciative of the North Pole and the South African tour guide was no exception. When I told him of this he was ecstatic and kept talking about it.

After Phinda we flew down to Port Elizabeth. I knew nothing of this area but Jacki had lived there a long time and she experienced what we all do when you knew something really well but hadn't seen it for years. She sort of recognised places but then said what would be next and it had moved or changed dramatically. Anyway, we arrived at her friend's house in the evening. We didn't know when we would arrive so that night they agreed that they would just arrange for us to have a few drinks at their house. I had thought nothing about this until we had been there a few minutes and Jenny said "I've warned my boss that Jacki is coming here from England and I will be very drunk tomorrow" and, so she was.

Port Elizabeth or PE as I had to call it was a strange place in that it was interesting to spend a couple of days there but there was nothing hugely interesting about the area. When we went from PE to Cape Town it was fantastic. We drove all the way there stopping at Knysna and, although we were on a major road, the sights were fantastic.

On arriving at Cape Town I immediately understood Jacki's comments. Cape Town was brilliant. The weather was far better than back home. To a large extent, we were still just basic tourists but it was clear that Cape Town is a huge area of cultural vitality and we were there for just a short trip before we got the flight back to Johannesburg.

When we were back in Johannesburg it was a couple of days before Christmas and we were going to spend it with Caroline's family so this required yet another drive. Christmas day was strange for me because firstly, I didn't know many people, but that doesn't matter and secondly,

I was in a new area and would like to have explored it but it was Christmas and we spent it as a family. The main thing I remember about Christmas was the lunch. In Britain, Christmas is in the middle of winter and cold so a large roast dinner is a great idea but in South Africa, it is in the middle of summer. The last thing you want is what I would call a Christmas lunch and so it was. Our Christmas meal was a large buffet and of predominantly cold food and it was fantastic. After having spent a couple of days there we went back to Johannesburg and then flew back to Britain.

Back in Britain we carried on as normal and I had booked a weekend away in Barcelona as Jacki was very keen on Spain and I hadn't been to Barcelona. The Barcelona trip was a disaster and nothing to do with Barcelona, rather Jacki had turned out to be in the very early stages of pregnancy and, unfortunately as we arrived in Barcelona, she started bleeding and lost the child. Regretfully she has been unable to get pregnant again.

Work was getting more and more difficult because I was basically the young Junior Partner in too small an office so I started looking seriously for other work and I ended up agreeing a job with a firm much nearer Salisbury, where I now lived with Jacki and it was the same size as Harris Walters which I had realised far better suited me. As a result, I gave my six months' notice to the firm and to my relief they said I had to work until the end of the month but then I was free to go on gardening leave. As I was on gardening leave I decided that I should travel a bit, as when I finished gardening leave, it would be back to work with a bang.

Gardening leave was fantastic as I was being properly paid to do nothing for a period of time. As far as booking holidays went, the first was a brief visit to southern Spain. Jacki's knowledge of southern Spain was excellent, whereas most people know of Malaga and Malaga alone she knew all the local places and was able to take us to fantastic places such as Ronda.

We tried going to Ronda twice but didn't make it up the mountain the first time. Ronda is at the top of a winding mountain and it takes an age to get to the top. The first time the weather at the bottom was superb, but as we got higher it became foggier and foggier. I decided that I couldn't get any higher and Jacki didn't want to continue so we had to decide to turn the car around and descend. Turning the car round wasn't that easy but eventually I found somewhere and turned the car round very slowly. The next day we decided to return to Ronda and see if we could make it to the top. The weather was perfect and it seemed a totally different route we were taking. I got straight up the mountain and it seemed in a fraction of the time to get part of the way, but it was clear and sunny. Getting there, it was well worth the trek. It was lovely. As a result of being so difficult to get to, it has remained untouched by the rest of the world. It sells all the modern things you need but shops are traditionally owned and run by the people who set them up or their families. The rest of the time we just did what we liked which was fantastic. We would visit places because we wanted to, but sooner than we thought, it was time to give back the hire car and return to the UK.

This current year was 2007 and the Rugby World Cup was being held in France. Both Jacki and I love rugby and I was a member of the England Supporters group so I decided to book the tickets for a couple of matches. The first was England against South Africa in the group stages and the other match was the final and we would just have to wait and see who would be playing who. We booked the tickets but before they would be played we had the wedding and honeymoon in Cape Town.

Both Jacki and I had been married before and, whilst we wanted our wedding to be seen we were not that worried about getting both families together, so we decided that we would go to Cape Town because we loved it. We would get married there right at the start of our holiday and then stay there on honeymoon. So we flew out overnight on the Saturday and arrived at Cape Town airport. We collected a hire car and got to the hotel where we were staying and all within about an hour of the plane landing, it was brilliant. The hotel decided that, as we were getting married, they would upgrade us so instead of just having a double room we had a suite which was wonderful. Having got there, the first thing we did was have a couple of beers and sit in the hotel's beach front garden overlooking the ocean. Although this was August and South Africa's winter, the sun was still there and this was just a magical few moments.

We had booked a wedding planner to arrange the wedding and had asked her to book the wedding on Table Mountain but when we rang her to confirm it, she wasn't too sure we would get up the mountain the following day. We could get married there but she wasn't sure when and we only had five guests but four were coming from elsewhere in South Africa. We knew that we had booked a wedding lunch at a vineyard, La Petite Ferme, in Franschhoek, a few kilometres from Cape Town and so we took the second option and decided to have the wedding there. In Britain, this would have caused no end of headaches but in Franschhoek it just happened.

The wedding was in itself fairly simple, but equally marvellous. There was a large duck pond area of the farm which would be uninterrupted for us throughout the wedding. After the wedding we would return to the main area of La Petite Ferme to sign the relevant documents, relax overlooking the vineyards, and then to have a fabulous wedding lunch. This aspect all appeared to be surreal probably because I know how difficult and expensive it would be in the UK, whereas there it was their duty to do what we wanted and the cost was incredibly low. Unfortunately Jacki's stepmother and her friend had to leave that day and so we had to get back from Franschhoek to Cape Town quite early and, soon enough, the mini bus had returned to collect us and take us back to Cape Town. We saw her stepmother and her friend off before collapsing in the hotel. We didn't know it beforehand, but we were tired so we had a quick sleep before contacting Jacki's friend and her husband, whom were our wedding witnesses, to see what they were doing in the evening. We decided we would go to their hotel for the evening and got a car from our hotel. We were staying in different hotels because we had booked them separately and they were leaving the following day, so we spent our wedding evening with them.

We went into their hotel restaurant and I think they had warned their hotel waiters that we had just got married because they swarmed all over us. When they were taking orders they made some fantastic suggestions including a vodka-based starter to Jacki's friend's husband where they didn't know why they marinated the starter in vodka, but it lit well, which was very exciting. When the starter was delivered they were pouring the vodka and it spilled, still lit! He got very upset and although he is an English-speaking South African they can always use the Afrikaans impolite words and he screamed that the vodka had got his 'tollie' which to us is his penis. After the meal he was trying to impress us with his knowledge of whisky but he didn't know Jacki and I had whisky at source, not South Africa. Whilst his knowledge was reasonable he lacked all the finesse about whisky and, it soon became clear, we knew more than him but fortunately he came clean and he had the whisky neat rather than drowning it with water as he had originally demanded.

We walked around the water front with them in the morning but then they got in their car and drove back to PE. This meant we were left alone as husband and wife for the first time. We decided that, for the afternoon, we would stroll around the Waterfront. The last time we were in Cape Town there was a jewellery shop in the Waterfront which had a white gold leopard necklace which was half price and Jacki had been disappointed that she didn't get it. I said if it was still there, she could get it. When we went into that area of the Waterfront Jacki was ecstatic to see the leopard necklace still there, but reduced by seventy per cent.

We were there for a total of three weeks and we were going to do exactly what we wanted to do and now that Jenny and Steve had left we were entirely on our own. We went watching sharks in a cage for a day which sounded fantastic but I am afraid it was a bit of a let-down. In many ways you actually did better watching from the boat rather than the cage. We also went up Table Mountain when we could and it was apparent that Franschhoek was the better place to get married but Table Mountain is fantastic, however too popular for a marriage.

We went back to Franschhoek a couple of times before we left and, in particular to the vineyard which we used for the wedding. Most of all, we were able to do what suited us best. Having a lounge in the hotel suite and overlooking the sea made the hotel a perfect place for us and we were quite happy if we were in the hotel for dinner and, if not dinner, then we would usually go to the bar for late drinks. One dinner, we decided to stay in the hotel and they produced the latest menu for us. We asked what the fish of the day was but this appeared to confuse the waiter and, eventually he announced that it is "silver fish sir"! I wasn't really sure what silver fish was but I ordered it and it was fantastic.

The start of the Rugby World Cup was whilst we were away and we managed to watch a bit of it on television over there. This was great as the South Africans were very knowledgeable about the sport and obviously they were supporting South Africa who was going to play England the second week of the tournament.

We arrived home knowing that we would be leaving again, this time for Paris and the England versus South Africa group match. We got to London and were going on the train under the channel tunnel. I had learnt the last time we went to Paris that Jacki was very nervous going under the tunnel and the best way to keep her calm was to have a bottle of champagne so I got Jacki and myself a bottle for the journey. Sitting opposite us and on the table to the side was a stag party going to the rugby. Apart from demanding champagne from us they were a hilarious group. When we arrived in Paris, we got details of the hotel and how to get to the stadium. At this point, we met them again, only by now they were well and truly drunk. Whilst they were going to the rugby I was not sure they knew what they had come to see. As we were waiting to go into the rugby a French female policeman approached them on horseback and one of them said you need to ride the horse carefully and then pranced around the horse saying "tippy, tappy, toe". The policewoman was fantastic as she was obviously told not to laugh and whilst keeping a straight face she did break open a smile.

The rugby itself was dire, at half time we were twenty points down. We were with all the England supporters except Jacki and a man who was wearing an England rugby top but was actually French and he was telling everyone around him that he was wearing a top because he had lost a bet on the France versus Argentina match. By half time, the only people making any noise in this section were those two. As the game went on, most people left the stadium but Jacki wanted to see the game out, and I admit, in a sad way so did I. Eventually, we lost thirty six to nil. At that stage, I thought we could see South Africa in the final but definitely not England. Going back into Paris we got on the Metro with a huge Afrikaans man. He was explaining that this had happened to England because Charles had left Diana for Camilla and because we called a man a sir when he was a madam, and then explained the Elton John situation to us. The people on the Metro were basically England supporters and they all accepted his humour and just laughed.

We got back home and watched the rest of the tournament from home. We knew England weren't out but no one could see them remaining in the tournament too long. South Africa was looking good. England finished second to South Africa so they had to play Australia in the quarter final and amazingly they won, only just, but they won. Everyone expected they would have New Zealand in the semi-final but New Zealand also lost to France. France was at home, so probably the favourites against England, but a try very early on gave England the win. I was going to a world cup final and England would play South Africa, this was brilliant.

We were at the stadium well in advance of the game and would go in as soon as they let us because we didn't want to miss a thing. Jacki received a text from her South African friend saying "where are you watching the game from?" Jacki replied saying "when we are let in we will go to our seat then". We thought we had told them we were going to the final but obviously she had forgotten because a text came back immediately saying "you bitch"! The text conversation went on with them trying to wind me up about the English chances, but then the gates opened and we walked to our seats. In the stand we were again in a white shirt area as I had got the tickets through the England Supporters Club but obviously Jacki was in green as were two people directly behind us. They had booked tickets when they knew South Africa were playing and had only managed to get these tickets.

This game was far better than the last game but, unfortunately, the result was another South African win. During the game, we had quite a chat to the two South Africans although they seemed to think I was quite stupid. It was not until Montgomery took a kick just before half time that this changed. Montgomery had appeared to have been limping a little bit and they started talking about taking him off but they trusted him with the last kick so I'm sure he was. There was a bit of controversy in the second half as to whether it was a try or not but, because it went to the video referee, his decision was accepted but from all bar three people in the area we were he got the decision wrong. Anyway, the result was a South African win and we were obviously going to see the presentation and wow it was good. Fireworks went off and the players were ecstatic, although the bit I remember was before when they brought out the trophy and a man came out of the stand and picked it up and waved it to the crowd before being escorted away from the scene by some not impressed officials.

The last thing we had to do before I was going to work for the new firm was a second wedding near Brighton so that the English people got to see us. My parents had booked a local restaurant near them where we had a room for all of us. Nothing else had been booked except a full meal and for some reason they had a cake there as well. The day was excellent as several people turned up including Jacki's mother whom I had not yet seen. Unfortunately Jacki's stepfather was feeling ill and couldn't make it but she had brought a friend with her. Beforehand, when we were deciding what to wear, Jacki had decided against wearing her wedding dress again but she did take it to show people what she wore and, not surprisingly, the girls all loved it and wanted to see it but the men were not that bothered. We had decided when we were in Franschhoek, we would have some of the wine we drank at our reception, shipped over and handed out. This was incredibly popular as, whilst in South Africa it cost virtually nothing, for England it was good wine. Shipping the wine actually cost more than the wine did! It was decided we would go back to my sister's house in Brighton to finish things off and we showed the video of the day but most people were looking at the back drop of Cape scenery rather than the reception.

Being back at work it became obvious that the work was not challenging enough for me and the only way I could be truly happy meant I had to change work. I had finally got myself sorted and had developed so that I was comfortably off and had the opportunity to increase this portfolio or so I thought.

10   The gap

I was now ready to go and start work for the other accountants and I don't know why, but I got conned and instead, we signed up for a property franchise. This was obviously a con but I bought into it and turned the other job down. Within two weeks it was blatant that this would not work and so I gave the franchise up. It was before I would have been due to start with the other firm and so I asked if they would reconsider but they said no.

This was disappointing, but not a surprise, but what happened the same day was a shock. It turned out that properties we had bought through property clubs were actually sold to us fraudulently and we had overpaid for them. I was a fully qualified Accountant but I would need debt advice. As it happened, a few days later a flyer for debt advice came through the door, so a second mistake occurred and I took the advice. The debt adviser was a local bankrupt but his boss was frequently on Radio Four and a respected member of the community.

With the debt problems waiting for a solution, we decided that I needed to get a job fast and probably we didn't think it through and Jacki and I ended up taking a job in Cape Town. This was a fantastic job as it would sort out our financial issues and we would live in Cape Town which, with all the places I have been to, is the most attractive place to live.

Unfortunately, this job was another disaster. The firm had a strong base in the Middle East and had set up in South Africa to develop the model in Africa. They were unaware of the regulations and that people who had moved to South Africa were likely to stay there so unfortunately we had to leave this job before our reputation got tainted. Unlike in Britain, we found getting a new job incredibly hard and I would meet people get on very well with them but when it came to working for them they were unprepared to do so.

Whilst we were in Cape Town there were a few things which were particularly good. Firstly as a Round Table member I thought it would be good to join the Cape Town Round Table. These were local Cape Town gentlemen and broadly similar to me. The one thing that really struck me about these men was the charity work they did was on a whole different level to us. Whilst we did fireworks and gave the money to local people they did similar things but gave it to aids victims, orphans and alike.

One Saturday, the Round Table had booked a table at a testimonial event for a local individual who had a rare type of cancer and had spent all his medical care would allow him. Jacki and I went to the event and it was fantastic. The cancer victim was there and he was so happy it was incredible and also frustrating as we knew in reality we were able to do nothing.

He was a keen rugby person and the local club had put this event on. To raise money one of the club members had grown his hair and had agreed he would have it cut off at this event which he duly did. By coincidence, I met him in the toilet, where he was talking to another guy about it and he said he had cut his hair but it wouldn't save the victim. I was very touched by this and I told the man not too worry and that he had done what he could and I shook his hand.

On one occasion I received an email inviting me to a book club. I had never been to a book club and this didn't look like one so I accepted but didn't know what for. The Chairman at Round Table had a quarterly male only braai. It was called a book club as a joke and the theory was that if a wife picked up on it you could say it was a meeting about books. This was great for me as it enabled me to meet local people, albeit men and talk to them. This was a great evening and I was invited to the next one but unfortunately we had left Cape Town by then.

The other thing I did, which was fantastic, is that I managed to get in touch with the three South Africans, who went to the North Pole with me, and one, in particular was in Cape Town and I agreed to go to his house for dinner. I was really looking forward to this as he was a great laugh as we got to the pole and also, because he was a former Springbok in rugby and had some great stories. In the end, I went for dinner at a restaurant with him as it turned out his wife was ill and they didn't want me to go to their house.

This was a great evening as there was a level of reminiscing about the North Pole and a level of looking forward. One thing he did mention was they had a photo of him and I and they showed it at the end of their presentation on the North Pole saying that anyone can go to the pole because this man, meaning me, did.

Whilst I was having a good time away from work the situation at work was quite dire and it looked like no amount of effort was going to result in Jacki or me staying there. There were a few bad words with Jacki, but unfortunately we had to leave Cape Town and I tried to get another job but couldn't get a job and we came home.

We went back home and had to stay at my parents as we didn't have anywhere to live and, whilst there, we had to get jobs as soon as possible. This was a painful few weeks as we wanted to get out of there as soon as possible but we needed to work, the good news was that we could get a job wherever we wanted as neither of us had a job or connections anywhere. The first job I heard about was an interesting job for me as it was a top 50 firm of accountants, just, but they dealt with my type of clients. These are owner managers of their business. I was delighted with getting an interview although Jacki was not too keen on having to live near Uxbridge.

The first interview I had was with a Partner at the firm and it sounded very positive. She actually said at one point that she couldn't believe it, I sounded just like I had come from their Partners' meeting. I knew I wanted the job but Jacki would need some persuading, still there was another interview to go. The amazing thing was, I had a phone call on the way back home to arrange a second interview once the Partner had spoken to the other Partners and they wanted me to bring Jacki so she could have a look around with the part-owner's wife, whilst I was with the other Partners.

She took Jacki to areas outside Uxbridge that were a bit nicer like Chalfont St Peter and Beaconsfield. This calmed Jacki enough for her to say that she would come with me if I got the job. I wouldn't be a Partner from day one, but then I couldn't be, given my financial situation, so a manager would be fine and they offered me that job at £10,000 more than they said. I had no problem with accepting this job.

It was all a rush, but at least this job meant I could gradually let my finances become clear but the first week I got a phone call about a job in Bahrain. This probably was not the best job but I would earn more money and tax-free. Whereas Barnes Roffe LLP was a job for life, Bahrain would be for five or six years and then back home. I was being employed at Barnes Roffe LLP three days a week so I had no problem in getting to London for the first interview and with a bit of luck I could also go to a second in Bahrain.

Jacki was keen to go to Bahrain in what she said to me but I don't think in reality she was. I pleaded with her for confirmation that I could go and she said yes so I agreed that from the 2nd of January I would start working with them in Bahrain. As I gave my notice to Barnes Roffe LLP, they were very upset and I wondered if I had made the right decision, but it was made and I would get ready for Bahrain.

We flew out to Bahrain and we had a couple of weeks in a hotel before having to rent a property but we weren't going to need to rent anywhere. After a couple of weeks, Jacki spoke to me and said she couldn't stay in Bahrain. This was Friday night. We decided to sleep on it but I knew I had to ring the part-owner at Barnes Roffe LLP and try to get my job back with him. I agreed with Jacki, if he said yes I would go back, but if he said no, then I was staying in Bahrain. I am not sure what she would have done, but I suspect that would have been the end of our marriage. I'd known the part-owner for a couple of months and now he may have inadvertently had a decision on our marriage.

11   Barnes Roffe LLP

I gave the part-owner a ring and he said he would have to speak to the other Partners but that he couldn't see a problem with it. He then rang me up a few minutes later saying there was no problem with me getting the job back. I agreed we would take a week or so to get back and that I would re-start a week on Monday.

The Monday came and we were leaving from Brighton to start work in Uxbridge. I couldn't believe how unfortunate things were and I had to ring in to say I would be a few minutes late because of traffic. Unfortunately, it had snowed overnight and, although we had left plenty of time to get back, refreshed and then drive into work the snow had caught us out. I was driving so Jacki rang to tell them but apparently only a few people knew I was coming back and so, although she told them, everyone thought I had left and didn't understand the message. I got back to the office and whilst I had lost one client to a fellow manager through thinking I had left I was able to get back to work as if nothing had happened.

The first couple of months it was simply just a case of managing jobs as they fell due and keeping on top of the jobs so that the part-owner could sign them off when he was ready. As a manager I was unable to sign accounts off, although having been a Partner before, I was able to get them to a finalisation stage. When I went to meetings with the part-owner I found it quite difficult as he was the Partner, but I wanted to say the Partner things. I soon learnt to let him talk about the accounts in general and then I could talk more about the specific issues. He was very perceptive and he knew that initially I would be quite happy not signing off on accounts but sooner or later I would want to. He couldn't make me a Partner because I had financial difficulties but instead he chose to make me a Responsible Individual and he gave me this job after about a year. This was a ridiculous title, but it is what the Institute calls a person who is allowed to sign accounts, but is not a Partner or Director if the firm is a company. This of course was of help to the part-owner, but I needed it as well.

Before all of this had happened, they also decided that one other Responsible Individuals and I would help out with the marketing of the company. This Responsible Individual was effectively on trial to become a Partner. The marketing was something I was looking forward to, I had come to enjoy it in the past and the North Pole trip had made me very relaxed about talking to people. The other Responsible Individual was reasonably good, but she was younger and far less experienced than me. I felt we added well to the outside selling team which was basically the Partners, Responsible Individuals and a marketing staff member.

The marketing was slow to develop, but the process was the same, get a contact and keep contacting them until they said yes, or regrettably no. It unfortunately is a fact of life that a couple of marketing wins will appear better than the best of accounting jobs but I got a few wins after a period of time.

Whilst most marketing was going to potential clients and trying to win them, there was also a seminar programme. We held various seminars throughout the year with a view to getting new clients and also keeping our existing clients. Originally, we had two seminar programmes, our own and a joint programme with a firm of lawyers and a local bank but regrettably we had to let the second programme go but not until I had done my first seminar to the groups' clients.

This evening I was giving my first seminar and I was a little bit nervous but, although it was my first seminar to the group, it was not the first time I had given this seminar. Still, when it came to speak, I found the people I knew and if I had any trouble I would look at them because they were in the crowd, so people would know I was looking at the crowd but they would leave it. Anyway, the seminar went well and now I could do some more. These were supposed to be quarterly seminars and we took them in turn to deliver so we should have had one every nine months, but this was our last seminar of the groups although we didn't know this at the time. Alongside these we had our own seminars, which I decided I would go to all of them and I managed to get picked to do a few, but it was one of a Partner's seminars that I had my biggest success at Barnes Roffe LLP. In the car park before a seminar, I parked up and another car parked next to me and it turned out the women was a target of ours and going to the seminar. We immediately connected and I decided to spend the seminar with her. I agreed a meeting with her and her boss which I went to with the part-owner and we signed them up, but the encouraging thing was that they wanted me to be their Accountant instead of the part-owner. Her boss was very wealthy and associated to other businesses which we subsequently also signed up.

During the term of working for Barnes Roffe LLP, Jacki decided that she would stop being an Independent Financial Adviser and would become a Nurse. She studied at Buckinghamshire New University and did her practical training at NHS Hillingdon Hospital and NHS Mount Vernon Hospital. She qualified in February 2013 and started work as a Community Staff Nurse near home.

As I had financial difficulties, there was no way I was going to be going abroad for holidays throughout this period, but I knew the Olympics were in London and I wished to be part of it. I sent out my form to become a Gamesmaker or, as I preferred, a Volunteer for the games. I went to my first selection process where we had to answer fairly routine questions and it actually went too well. The only real problem I had with working during the games was only taking the games off as holiday and not extra time. At the selection session I realised that the woman was very impressed with me and she asked me how long I had and I said I am afraid it is only the games and a few occasional days as well. She decided I hadn't said that and put down to be given to a national Olympic Committee and become responsible for ensuring that their athletes and officials get where they want to be and on time. This sounded fantastic to me. I would be based in the Olympic Village and spend a lot of time with the athletes, but unfortunately, after I went to a couple of training sessions it became clear I would need a full six weeks available which I just couldn't do.

Regrettably, I had to reject this role, but I made it clear I would still like something for the games themselves. I was getting impatient because I had heard nothing, but eventually it came through and I was asked to work in Earl's Court for the volleyball and, in particular, I was in the mobility section. Our job was to help disabled people to the games and make sure they saw the games in comfort. This wasn't the first role I was offered but it was a job for the games and it was great fun.

The first day I was there it was a woman's day and one of the first people I met were the family of the American volleyball captain and her grandmother had tickets for all of America's matches and she was in a wheelchair. I had a nice chat with them as I took her to her seat and then got on with my job, but a few minutes later I saw her daughter coming back down the corridor and looking to go out, so I spoke to her. Their tickets were fine but there was a male with them who was also the National Head of the sport and he had brought the wrong day's tickets. I went to find him outside and consider going for special consent to get in, but, actually by the time I got to him, he had bought tickets from a tout and got in that way. Over the course of the games I got to know these people fairly well as they came for the American matches only. In this phase, you got a ticket for two games at a time but they would not worry about the second match.

During our stay at our rental house the official agent of the landlord had been taking banking's for the landlord and keeping them himself rather than giving them to the landlord, most noticeably with the deposits. We weren't directly involved by this and so we only got the second hand comments from people but he had a letting agent premises in Chalfont St Peter and it very suddenly closed and our agent disappeared. I was not sure exactly what happened, but the police were definitely looking for him and we received an email from our landlord.

The e-mail basically said that they had lost their deposit and possibly a bit of rent and that they had given the property to a new named agent to run. Actually, whilst this was a bit stressful at the time, it was quite good news for us. It wasn't our money as he was the landlords' agent, and the new agent had no knowledge of what happened so actually played a straight bat with us. Perhaps one of the worst things to happen in this time was that our boiler broke. We had tried getting annual safety checks of the boiler, which eventually we got, but they said that because of the way the cupboard had been made around it he couldn't check certain things with the boiler. In January, during a very cold spell, we started getting some minor problems with the boiler. When a repair man came around he firstly removed the cupboard we had been told couldn't be removed and then shut down the boiler on safety reasons.

Getting the boiler repaired took far longer than was necessary because the repair man was trying to keep the landlords happy. Rather than just replacing it he kept on trying to repair it for the landlords. Eventually, they had to replace the boiler but, unfortunately, they had wasted three weeks and that was three weeks of the worst weather we had had for a few years.

During the year, my finances looked like they were getting back to the state before the property fraud and I began thinking about becoming a Partner at Barnes Roffe LLP. The outside world had worked in my favour over the past few years and I was going to clear the potential liabilities on me and then I could become a Partner, or at least, so I thought. I was having an appraisal and I thought the part-owner had told me that it had been decided that I would not become a Partner there to which I was very upset and started thinking about where my next job would come from. I had a contact with jobs in Australia and New Zealand and I called her that evening.

Every so often, when it was a Friday, we took our better clients out for lunch and it became quite a heavy lunch. I am not sure what was said but a client of mine picked up I was dissatisfied at the firm and took it out on the part-owner. It was the evening now and we were all heavily drunk, but the part-owner took me aside and asked me what was going on to which I replied "I want to be a Partner and, if it is not available, I will leave" and he said "what about from the 1st of January 2013?" which I naturally accepted. He warned me the other Partners needed to agree, but if he wanted a Partner the others would normally agree. I had the formalities of becoming a Partner to complete and these included doing two speeches at the Partners meeting and I went to the October and November 2012 meetings to give my speeches. After the November meeting I was officially appointed as a Partner from January 2013.

We had a great Christmas knowing I would become a partner and Jacki was just about to finish her nursing studies and my financial problems were disappearing so the next year, we would really be able to enjoy. At least, that was the plan.

12   28th April 2013

It is incredible, but this day has completely changed my life. However, I don't really know what happened. I would like to make myself look good by saying it turned out to be positive but the fact is, it was bad. There are a few good points such as having a Blue Badge for the car, but they are insignificant when one considers I have had to give up work, or even the fact that I now need to have a blue badge. I will now report how I remember the stroke and then report exactly what those snippets mean in real life.

On Friday 26th April 2013, before I went to work, I saw Jacki had entered a note on the calendar saying that I had done something twice whereas I had only done it once. This annoyed me a bit as I drove to work. I remember that we went out for a group lunch, I think because it was our Receptionist's birthday and I think we went to the Black Horse which was just about a local for the office. I can't remember what I had or when we came back.

The next thing I remember was later that evening I had a row with my wife and stormed out of the house. I drove to the end of the road and then drove back and re-entered the house. Jacki had gone upstairs and locked herself in the bedroom so I went outside again and programmed the satnav to Beachy Head near Eastbourne. There was no intent to harm myself but I have never seen Beachy Head, so I started driving.

The next thing I am aware of is, close to Beachy Head where I was following the road directions, my satnav was now saying I was there and I followed them to a point which said you are now at Beachy Head, but it was well within land and nothing like the cliffs I expected. I left, a bit disappointed and just as I left Beachy Head, I saw a strange looking young couple in an old VW Beetle looking at me intently and oddly.

I then recall turning into the road where I lived but I saw that a lot of people were in my house and I didn't want to disturb a party so I turned back around and went off. The next thing I knew, I was walking along some country lane when a weird looking man came past me in a 1950's style open top van. I mean open top because it didn't even have a windscreen and he was strange. The only thing I remember about him was that he had a beard that was down to his waist and no hair at all, including eyebrows. I don't remember what he was talking about but he was saying something.

After that, I don't know any of the dates, but I do remember once waking up somewhere I didn't know and asking a kind young lady where the toilet was. I awoke a second time to watch some football but I don't know who the game was between or anything that happened. I also went home once and had a look at the schedule that had been changed and it had been torn out of the file.

Well, I am afraid that is all I can remember about two and a bit weeks of my life. I have written 452 words about the most significant two and a bit weeks of my life and those words are mostly rubbish, although they are almost true, the exact detail is often vastly different. If I now repeat what happened as I know from talking to other people, you will see how woeful my memory is because other than what is in those words, as far as I am concerned, nothing else happened.

So, the beginning of the year was excellent for us. Although I started a new job, officially I had been doing it anyway. There were some noticeable changes in that I now shared an office with the part-owner, although the way our job is I think we were only a few times in there together. I also needed a new car as mine didn't have the aura of a Partner about it and it was old. From a job viewpoint, I had progressed externally but actually the job hadn't really changed.

Jacki, on the other hand, had a major change in that now she was a qualified Nurse, recruited to do community nursing and she started this in April. Jacki was beginning to get into the swing of nursing when I had the stroke, in fact she hadn't had her first payslip when I had the accident and, unfortunately, she was booked off sick with stress as a result of my stroke. Her job in North West London regrettably had to be left, more or less, as it begun. This is a big regret of mine and I am pretty sure Jacki feels the same way, although she won't say.

The beginning of 2013 was an exceptional time for us only it was going to change dramatically and, in essence, suddenly on the 28th April 2013. On the Saturday, apparently I had been doing domestic chores including mowing the lawn and I decided to go for a drive in the evening. I am not really sure why I had decided to drive and sometimes I wonder what would have happened if I had stayed at home but, at the end of the day what happened did happen and I can never reverse the clock and change it.

At around nine o'clock, I was picked up by the ambulance and it was clear I had a small amount of hypothermia but fundamentally I was all right. Jacki went to the hospital, NHS Wexham Park Hospital and gradually got other people around me to visit, including a Partner from work and the part-owner's wife. Apparently, I was perfectly all right at this point of time and I commented that I would have the surgery on my jaw and then I will be back and fighting fit again.

Jacki said I would not be in for a few days and was delighted when they both turned up on the Sunday to visit me in Accident & Emergency. The part-owner could not be there as he was away from the area so he sent his wife. She also worked at Barnes Roffe LLP and so did know who I was. At this stage, I had not yet had the stroke, so we all thought it would be fine and once I'd had a few days recuperating, I would be back at work. That was going to change very quickly.

At about three o'clock, I started going odd and my demeanour changed dramatically. Jacki knew something was going wrong but could not tell exactly what it was. I was totally uncomfortable with what was happening and my speech went horribly wrong. Firstly, I was using the wrong words, then speaking gibberish and eventually I could make no sense at all. After this I wet myself as I could no longer control my bladder, and it was this that particularly upset Jacki.

The Partner there was real god send throughout this process, and I knew from her job as a Partner that she had the determination to find a way through any problem, but probably Jacki did not. As the day developed and I started going downhill Jacki was very impressed by the Partner's determination and when Jacki and her mother became aware that I was beginning to slip into a stroke despite the hospital's refusal it was this Partner who was getting the most annoyed. She insisted Jacki did something about it on the Sunday afternoon and she herself threatened to sort it out if Jacki could not but still they couldn't get interest out of the hospital.

This was probably at around five o'clock, but when you spoke to the doctors who were responsible for me there was no concern. Their opinion was I was just 'in shock'. At the end of the day, one doctor actually told Jacki it was just my way of dealing with it. She met him on her way out of the hospital, on her way home and said what do you think is wrong with him and he looked at her and said it is just 'shock'. Jacki was ecstatic about this because, yes it was messy and undignified behaviour, but it was going to be dealt with and she could go home to sleep.

The next morning Jacki got up and went to the hospital where she saw one of the doctors looking very concerned about me. She asked him what he was thinking and he said it appeared I had had a stroke and it then transpired it had happened with them watching at the hospital in Accident & Emergency. I was sent for an MRI scan to confirm this. Regrettably it was confirmed I'd had a stroke and I went back to the ward, only this time instead of the Orthopaedic ward, I went back to a specialist Stroke Unit and I was put into the high care section for specialist attention.

I obviously don't remember the next few days but I have picked the following things up over time. Apparently, I was unable to walk to start with but I did manage to climb the safety barriers on my bed the first night in the orthopaedic ward. We didn't discover this for months as Jacki was not informed about it, which annoyed her and I also think she would have been encouraged by my endeavours to escape even if that wasn't the best option.

The next thing that Jacki had to deal with was my family coming to visit me. The first visitation was from my mother, driven up by my brother-in-law. I don't really know what happened but Jacki obviously didn't get on with my mother and she now refuses to see anyone from my family at all, although she does allow and even encourages me fully to see them. Jacki reports that it took them a long time to come and see me but their viewpoint is that they had the police report that I was in hospital but that I was going to be let out in a couple of days so they didn't bother coming to see me. It was only when they had a phone call from Jacki's cousin reminding them of the seriousness that they realised something was up. When they arrived, Jacki was told by the Stroke Unit that my mother had removed Jacki as next-of-kin off the file. My mother adamantly denies this and it is probably a hospital mix up but it has stuck with Jacki.

My mother came quite rapidly in the beginning, but my two sisters did not. They only came up many days later when I was in the Stroke Unit, although I was unaware of this. Jacki has taken great delight in telling me that my oldest sister asked me "had told me how that I was brain damaged yet?" and apparently even her husband was embarrassed by this. Jacki was livid and took immediate action to clear the air but it made no difference anyway as I could not remember this.

Although I cannot remember any of this apparently Jacki had a busy first few weeks at the hospital. The first thing she had to do was make sure I was alright, at least as far as possible. Every day I needed to get up and this was not as easy as one would think. I did not know what was involved or how much should be done so I had to rely on Jacki to make sure I was up each day, and she would make sure I was wearing appropriate clothes. I wasn't worried what I wore so that when the nurses set me up in the green hospital pyjamas that they had on the ward I simply took them with no questions. However, once Jacki saw them she was very annoyed as she had been bringing in fresh, clean clothes each day and she was not amused if I was not wearing them. She was of the view that I would not be able to get my head around the problem if I was used to being in hospital clothes, and she was probably right, as there were clothes there for me to wear I ought to be dressed in them for the day.

Jacki was not happy and reported this to the Matron and, apparently they were so concerned about what she may do, that her and her mother who had come to stay with her for the week were entertained by the Ward Sister with teas and biscuits. Whilst Jacki was amused by this, it didn't solve the problem itself, although it was made clear to the nursing staff to always make sure that during the day I was dressed in my own clothes.

As I mentioned, Jacki's mother came down for the first week I was in hospital although I didn't even know this. She was brought up by a friend of hers and she stayed for the entire first week which I believe helped Jacki no end. I didn't know how tough this was for Jacki and all I can do is imagine it, so at least having her mother to whinge and moan at must have been good. It is true what they say about your partner's needing more help than you as, firstly, I knew nothing about what was happening and secondly, I had huge amounts of care and assistance from the general staff.

Throughout the first couple of weeks or so I was unable to walk and had to be got in and out of bed by a hoist. I couldn't even sit up straight in a wheelchair. I cannot imagine how horrible this was for me and for Jacki. At least I know nothing about this, whereas Jacki knows the full detail of how bad it was. Fortunately, it only lasted a couple of weeks and when I was up and aware of what was happening there was no way it would happen again. With the usage of hoists it meant that bathing me was also a problem and Jacki decided to help the nurses by giving me a bed bath and by cleaning my naked body.

By now, I was well entrenched in the Stroke Unit and my main consultant seemed to be very helpful, when I actually saw him and, earlier he provided Jacki with a lot of useful information. Whilst he gave lots of disclaimers about his thoughts they more or less came good. He told Jacki that I should walk again and that the stroke probably hadn't affected my intelligence, but I would find speech very difficult. Even now, he is right about the speech. I know what I want to say but can't think of the right words and by the time I do the conversation has moved on and normally I just don't bother to say anything if there are a few or more people involved.

Apparently, they had me doing some physical training in order to get myself ready for when I left hospital and went home. I had a few sessions once I was conscious but I also had them before and Jacki went to watch a few. I wasn't very impressed with these physiotherapy sessions and, as soon as their back was turned, I would stop whatever they had given me to play with. Having said that, according to Jacki, there was one occasion when a girl came in with a book that she just read rather than trying to help me. This sort of training is a good idea but it does need commitment from both parties. Once I was conscious, I was committed and this seemed to have the desired effect on the staff and, although I didn't have that much in the way of tuition, at least I had some. Most of their ideas were a lot too old for me, probably because I was a lot younger than other stroke victims.

At the time of the accident, I was a member of BUPA through work and the partnership insisted and Jacki agreed we would look into me being transferred to a BUPA hospital to get on with intensive rehabilitation. The Wellington in London was chosen but Jacki was talked out of it by NHS Wexham Park. Also, BUPA would only agree to me being in their hospital twenty one days and she thought I would need a lot longer. The NHS hospital was very against it which surprised Jacki and when I was told me as well. It would appear that they had some sort of budgetary constraint against me moving which struck me as a bit weird as I would have thought that if I became a private patient that would be better for the NHS. By the time I was conscious this had been resolved as me remaining with the NHS although occasionally we still wonder if that was the right thing to do.

It seemed like Jacki had huge amounts of things to do in the first few weeks since the accident as she also had to deal with the police, a variety of insurance companies mainly the car but also the critical illness cover and also get me a Blue Badge for when I went home. These all started whilst I was I non compos mentis, although they continued whilst I was still in hospital and in some cases a lot longer.

I had to feel a bit sorry for the police as they were left to tidy up the mess that I had made and Jacki took this whole job to heart which I was very impressed with. Allegedly, I had ended up being parked in a local farmyard and firstly they had to arrange for someone to collect the car and take it to their pound but then they had to inspect it to see if there had been anything suspicious with the car. Obviously, the only suspicious activity was my driving and there had been no tampering with the car.

Once they had inspected the car, then Jacki had to go and collect anything that was in the car. She was advised not to take a look at the car but Jacki is curious and there was no way she wouldn't look. When she looked, at first she over stepped the car, not even realising it was a Nissan 370Z until she was told. It was a terrible sight and Jacki fell to her knees when she realised that this was the car. Even now, she does not know how I managed to get out alive.

It is amazing to think that these were all dealt with at least initially in my absence although I did manage a few signatures later on, although they looked nothing like my signature. Jacki dealt with all of the initial phases although a lot of them did query my lack of involvement in making the claim, insisting that as I was insured it should be me that makes the claim. They usually only tried this once as Jacki had got very good at responding to them and asking if they could make me say anything that made sense. Being asked so directly the answer was of course no, so they would just send a claim form. I wasn't brilliantly insured but there were a few sums that came through, specifically the critical illness cover I had, so a few things got sorted which was fantastic given that I would have nothing except for benefits in the future.

Perhaps one of the easiest things she had to do but also one of the most important was to get me a disabled badge. We didn't know it at the time but the UK registration is in Beaconsfield which was very near to where we live. As it was so close, Jacki decided to go in face to face rather than speak to them over the phone. When she was in there, she met a South African girl working for the company and she got on with Jacki like a house on fire. Jacki told the girl what had happened to me and she, without hesitation, said that I could have a Blue Badge but they needed a photograph of me. She asked if Jacki could take a photograph of me but Jacki realised that my head was twice its' normal size from the accident and covered in bruises, so any photograph would be useless, but she remembered my passport. The girl agreed to try scanning in the passport photograph which she managed to do and it worked. It was now just a question of time before it came. I was still in hospital for a few weeks when it arrived in the post.

It was obvious I had become aware that I was in hospital, although I do not remember this, as when I first got back to what I consider being conscious I somehow knew where I was without having to make a formal inspection of the place. This was sort of weird, because I was somewhere which should have felt unusual with people who would have been strange to me, yet I knew it and them, although I couldn't explain why. In fact, I do vaguely remember gaining my faculties and remember I woke up, but was not where I expected to be. I was in a big, but single bed, which had all sorts of contraptions around it and was nothing like my own warm and cosy bed which I thought I had got into last night. I was awake but something was very wrong I didn't know where I was and, more importantly, why I was there.

This is something I would consider more but, for now, I needed the toilet. I decided to walk to the bathroom and as I extracted myself from the bed I realised, firstly, I had a corpse's tunic on as if he had just died in hospital and, secondly and more importantly, I had no idea where the bathroom was. In addition to this, I was very ginger on my feet. The art of getting out of bed probably took quarter of an hour and I had no idea why.

Once I was out of bed, I looked around the room for some more information. The bed looked equipped for every sort of incident and there was also a basin, a couple of chairs and a small storage cupboard but nothing told me where I was. I decided I had to go to the loo first and this was going to be a problem as I still didn't know where one was. Nonetheless, I decided that I must leave the room and see if I could find one.

Ultimately, I made my way to the only door in the room and bravely tried to open it, but unfortunately it was locked, or at least that was what I thought. I couldn't see anything that could lock the door. There was no key hole or anything like that. The door wouldn't open and eventually I gave up and by now, was desperate for the toilet, so against my better judgement I decided to go in the sink. I tried to start the taps running but again they would not turn and after a couple of minutes I was exhausted and just collapsed onto the bed. It was strange because, although I felt exhausted after about ten minutes, I was fully alright again.

I felt the taps were too tight so I decided I would try to loosen them by trying one tap with both hands and as I did the tap gradually began to move and it started trickling and I felt it would come further but it was still jammed, but a trickle was enough to allow me to go to the toilet and I took great delight in reliving myself albeit in a basin, but once that was done I could begin thinking about where I was and escaping back to my own home. This is how I remember things, but clearly it is not the case as Jacki reminded me I was catheterised.

I decided to have a look in the small storage cupboard and I found my own wallet and a few clothes that I also recognised as mine. Perhaps the most satisfying thing was a small collection of photographs of me at the North Pole and then it finally clicked that I was in hospital but still did not know why. Just as I realised where I was, the door opened and a Nurse came in, obviously expecting me to be lying in my bed. She was shocked and ran out before I had a chance to question her. The North Pole photographs gave me great satisfaction as firstly, they meant Jacki had been there although she wasn't at the moment and secondly, it gave me good memories of myself.

I heard nothing from the Nurse for few minutes and again she locked the door but then the door opened and it was Jacki who had been contacted by the nurse as I regained my own thoughts after about two weeks and I was alive, if not how I knew it.

Over the next few days, I came into consciousness fully and I am delighted to say I have been that way since and I knew I had to wait until Jacki arrived at the hospital before fully understanding what had happened to me. When she arrived, I started to speak to her, and I am not sure whether this was normal to her or not but to me it was very different. I had lost about eighteen days and I don't know if I spoke sense, but at least I now knew I was speaking. I thought I would make sense up to a point but I was aware that my diction was stunted and that often, I would want to use one word but had another word come out of my mouth which I could not correct, even though often I knew it was wrong.

The hospital soon got to know I was conscious and they decided to give me certain tests to determine which of my assets were still there. I thought I could walk properly, although the hospital did not, but whilst I was in hospital I only went small distances so couldn't tell.

My main concern was how cognitively impaired I was and even now there are several things which catch me out. The first test they gave me was a sheet of very simple numerical calculations which I would normally have laughed at. It involved simple things like one plus two. Despite being simple, I didn't get one correct, but the hospital seemed to expect this and the next day gave me a sheet of complex calculations to do and I got them all nearly right. The complex calculations were tough, in fact most people who visited me refused to try them.

The objective testing girl actually thought I had a calculator to complete them but I was just using my head. The first sheet was obviously given to me just to get my brain used to doing calculations again, as the hospital didn't worry about my results and then gave a very hard version to me. Even now, I do not fully understand this, but my calculations are not quite as good as they used to be but almost, although I have difficulty remembering where I am with a calculation.

I was also given language tests which told me what I knew in that my language was fine but I didn't have much in the way of a memory so names were a real problem to me. In fact they still are. I have lost count of how often I have called Jacki by my ex-wife's name. I am getting better at it now, but especially when I am angry, I still call her by this wrong name. She has gone for me a few times when I have called her this but she clearly knows it is a problem with me, so normally leaves it. At least now I usually realise before I have said anything.

It seems the amount of tests they gave me was inconsequential to the amount of time I was in the hospital, but they kept me pretty much fully occupied during the days when I was in hospital. I think the lack of energy I have to take on even the smallest task has been the hardest thing to deal with, but again obviously the hospital was aware of this.

I had been in hospital just over a month now and I had deliberately grown a beard as I knew I had broken my jaws in five places and I didn't want to touch it as I thought I could do it even more damage. Clearly the doctor didn't agree with me but he seemed afraid to tell me. I was coming up to the operation so he had to tell me and when I then said why I hadn't been touching it because of being scared to he just said "oh, I had never thought of that!" I immediately went to the sink and started to take my beard off as I didn't really like it but I was, until then, too afraid to shave it. He assured me that my jaws would have healed where they were and, whilst it may be difficult to shave, I was extremely unlikely to do anything to my jaws although I did cut myself a lot and quite badly.

I got myself relatively clean shaven and they came around to give me tests for facial mandible surgery which confused us as we were expecting them to be planning to move me to a rehabilitation hospital first. Jacki was more annoyed than I was but that is probably because she was truly aware of the situation whereas I was just living for the next minute all the time. Now the hospital had arranged for me to have a metal jaw piece inserted in my bottom jaw and this would be in a couple of days' time. I would need some recuperation time so instead of going straight to a rehabilitation hospital, it looked like I would still be at NHS Wexham Park Hospital for at least a week. They could also not tell us which rehabilitation hospital I would be going to which needed planning by Jacki to get to in the first instance as she was with me every day.

The day of the surgery came and everyone about me seemed to be panicking a little bit and I thought I was the only calm one there but, as the surgery started, I very soon realised it was that they knew what the surgery was. I still had my rose coloured spectacles on and I was under the impression that, if it was dangerous, the hospital wouldn't do it but that isn't how hospitals work. The fact is, any operation they do is dangerous and above all it can hurt. Furthermore, I was a very high risk patient because I had a clot caused by the accident which inevitably caused the stroke.

Before I was due to go for surgery, Jacki came in and she had brought her friend with her. They had trained together as Nurses. Before the operation, they sat around my bed and just talked and talked. I have no idea what they said as I tried sleeping for a few minutes and also, I didn't know who or what they were talking about and so I just let them get on with it and I would worry about my operation. Every so often they would ask what I thought about certain things and I would either just smile at them or, if I really had no clue, I would pretend I was asleep.

Eventually, the time came for me to be taken to the theatre. I was quite amazed, but whilst I was waiting for the surgery they had allocated two staff to go with me although I think one was a student. It impressed me that I had to go with two people and at this stage I was still unaware of what was happening. They waited with me and, because Jacki and her friend were not allowed to follow me into the theatre, I was forced to say goodbye to them first and Jacki seemed genuinely worried. The time eventually came and I went into surgery with what appeared a very laid-back team. I assume they weren't, but they appeared to be fully aware of what was happening and totally unfussed by the surgery, which I must admit made me feel a lot better. Obviously, I don't remember much about the surgery but I do remember at the end when they were due to transport me back to my bed the tall one said "remember the base height is the smallest person" and then positioned his hands by his ankles to make fun of the smallest person.

After the surgery, I went back to a recovery area so they could keep a close eye on me and when they were happy, I went back to the stroke ward. I have a feeling Jacki caught me as I was going to the recovery area and asked if I was alright. I nodded, but by the time I had really worked out what was going on I had passed her and I was in the post operation room. I don't know how long I had to wait here but it was probably about two hours and basically everyone who had been connected to the operation had to come and make sure that their bit of the operation had worked. I think the work they did to check the operation was sensible and needed doing, but I must admit it just annoyed me as all I wanted was to get back to my ward and then sleep.

I wanted to get back to my ward and sleep, well at least that is what I tried, but the fact is I was in agony and, whilst I tried to sleep I spent most of the day in bed. I was awake just trying to accept the pain my mouth and jaw were suffering. Overnight, I must have woken up about ten times and each time I pressed my buzzer. I had seen this buzzer every day I was in hospital but never felt the need to use it, but I did now and I used it. Every time I awoke, I was in some pain with my jaws and I called the Nursing staff in the hope they had the proper painkillers.

There was one Nurse who I am still convinced gave me the wrong person's drugs as, after she had left, my pain multiplied and the agony became unbearable. I mentioned this to Jacki expecting her to go mad but she just laughed at me. Eventually, I told a member of staff with Jacki there but they were of the opinion that it was just the situation and it was unfortunate my agony rose as soon as she left but that the painkillers were as good as could be expected and I suppose I have to believe them.

The pain remained until the next morning and it was quite strange, the pain was there and at a relatively high level, then it just appeared to stop suddenly. Once it stopped, it then stopped forever and just left me with a metal plate in my mouth which, as far as I can tell, will be there as long as I am around.

I had missed going to a rehabilitation hospital because of the operation and I still needed to recuperate in NHS Wexham Park Hospital for another week or so. The nice thing about NHS Wexham Park Hospital is that I was in my own room, but unfortunately they now needed the room for a critically ill patient and, whilst they had considered me to be critical previously, they no longer did and I got removed from this room into a general ward. To start with, it didn't bother me and at least now I could walk around and, providing I told the nurses where I was going, I was free to wander around the hospital so initially I survived the general ward but quite soon it got too much for me.

In the ward everyone was ill, particularly the person who was opposite me. I was in this ward about a week and I don't think he moved in all that time. He was kept alive by drips and every so often the Nurses would come and close his curtains around his bed and treat him and then he was back in exactly the same place. I don't know what was wrong with him and whether or not he made it out of the hospital but I can say he looked incredibly unwell. Being in this sort of general ward just made me feel ill and depressed which I had managed to ignore when I was in the single room.

I had been there some time and they told me that, providing I told them where I was going and returned for certain times, I could go about the hospital. Knowing I could do this was fantastic, but actually I never really wanted anything, so didn't worry about it too often. One day, I was really depressed and visiting hours were not until two o'clock, but it was about quarter to two and I could tell Jacki had already arrived. If Jacki tells you she will be with you by two o'clock she will be there at the very latest at two o'clock so I told the Nursing staff I was going and we went round the hospital and got a cup of coffee.

The most enjoyable thing about doing this was the fact that other people were also there early and they just had to wait. Even so, I was still distressed by the current place on the Stroke Unit and managed to persuade Jacki to come in the evening as well because, although she could come twice a day, she usually only came the once but this time I wanted her back in the evening. It is not really acceptable to feel like that but I was actually quite depressed by my situation. I was just coming to terms with never working again and I was still stuck in that hospital. Throughout my time at NHS Wexham Park Hospital, I was reasonably happy with the level of visits I had. Pretty much all of the office staff had come at one point or other. In particular, my fellow Partners came. A few clients had also managed to find their way there, but what had really impressed me, was the number of cards I received from people which was fantastic. Now that I have been absent for over two years and I have to accept that no one is truly indispensable.

I spent a couple of extra days in this hospital as they were waiting for a place at a rehabilitation hospital, ideally NHS Amersham Hospital, to have a free bed. Finally, the day came when I was due to leave for NHS Amersham Hospital and I spent the entire day waiting for patient transport to come and take me. The transport eventually arrived at about six o'clock and they wanted me to go in a wheelchair. I have tried to pretend that my walking is not affected by the stroke, but I have to accept that it is definitely worse than before I had the stroke. Even now, I get tired quickly but then a few steps on my own and I was gone so I was forced into a wheelchair and I just had to accept it.

Well, they may have arrived late but they didn't hang about with driving. The driver had his assistant; myself and someone who looked very ill laid out lengthways on an ambulance bed. They took him where he had to go first which I think it was acceptable, given he appeared to be very ill. They then drove me the back way to NHS Amersham Hospital and the driving was fast, or at least that is what it appeared to me. He was tearing around corners in his ambulance at speeds I would have been worried about in the sports car.

When I arrived, Jacki who had been with me up until I left at NHS Wexham Park Hospital, had already made it there as she didn't need to drop anyone off. I was very pleased she was there to start with as I knew nothing and, more importantly, I thought I knew all I needed to. I arrived quite late at night so they basically settled me in for the night and gave me a quick welcome, but the fact is I was very tired and all I wanted to do was have a coffee and then fall asleep. The Healthcare Assistant was about to offer me a biscuit with my coffee which rarely happened and, although I knew better, I would have accepted but then saw I was still on pureed food because of my fractured jaws. We left it then, but Jacki decided we would get them to remove this pureed food regime as they had done so, albeit just, at NHS Wexham Park Hospital.

Perhaps the best thing about NHS Amersham Hospital was that the bed next to me was occupied by a man who was quite a bit older than me and had also had a stroke, but his was bad. Whilst he could talk reasonably well, everything else he needed assistance with. I feel quite cruel about this now, but looking at him made me feel good because, what had happened to him could have happened to me. He was a genuinely nice man which was probably just as well because he was going to need a lot of friends and allies.

Sleeping next to him made me fully aware of what could have happened. A stroke is very bad and you have it for the rest of your life but at least I can walk and go to the toilet myself. Appreciating walking was very important to me, because whilst I was at NHS Wexham Park Hospital, I was annoyed about my walking as I couldn't think about the North Pole again, in fact if I walked twenty or thirty yards I had to stop and get some energy back but I could be left alone, which was fantastic. The toilet had never been a problem and I didn't even consider it could be a problem but having seen my companion next to me, it made me think there is always someone worse than me.

I never said anything about this to anyone, but I guess everyone knew. I knew my thinking was going to have to change from then on as there is always someone better than me to there is always someone worse than me. This would take some time for me to completely come to terms with, but I do have it for the vast majority of time and there is no doubt it is why I am surviving.

I thought the idea of going to NHS Amersham Hospital was meant to be about dealing with the recuperation aspect a little bit more than at the main hospital and, to some extent that was true. The fact that I could walk a little bit, with help and was just about alright in terms of washing myself, meant they didn't really have that much to do for me and as soon as I arrived, they were looking to send me home.

The first full day at NHS Amersham Hospital and Jacki had decided I was going to eat normal food from that day on. Being a hospital, it is not as simple as just saying a person doesn't need pureed food anymore. It needs to be proven by a series of seemingly irrelevant tests. Firstly, I had someone look at my mouth and throat without any obvious tools and say that they thought I could eat normal food. After that, I had a second test with someone different where I ate a normal meal in front of them. As I didn't choke or splutter they signed me off and I could then eat normally again. My jaws were still broken so I had to steer clear of some very chewy things, but the rest was good news.

The second full day I was there, someone who was dressed immaculately in white said that I could only have a shower every other day and rely on a basin wash the rest of the time. Reluctantly, I agreed with him that day and had a basin wash although I did make sure it took even longer than a shower so that I proved this was not happening again. He was dressed immaculately so I assumed he was a doctor but I actually found out he was a Healthcare Assistant so I am not sure if he should have said that or not. I chose to ignore the comment about showering every other day and did shower every day and, although I made no secret of this, he never mentioned it again.

The first weekend I was in NHS Amersham Hospital they let me out for the Saturday afternoon providing I didn't go very far and Jacki was with me permanently. The two constraints were irrelevant as my first time in the real world for well over a month it was obvious I would be with Jacki and we wouldn't travel far. We spent the afternoon itself in Amersham. Something we had never really done, despite living a few miles from Amersham. I don't remember much of what we did but it was just fantastic to be outside and free again. Although I did have to go back, we now knew they were going to let me out for good very shortly.

I do remember a couple of things. Firstly, I remember how slowly we did everything. Prior to the stroke, we would have walked around Amersham in a couple of hours and stopped if we had wanted to, but now it took three or four times as long and I made sure we stopped frequently and I do mean, frequently. It took some getting used to how slow it was and I still struggle a bit but that is partly why I can no longer work. One such stop was at the old park where a band was playing old tunes for those listening. I remember thinking I would never have come to an event like this before, but I had to stop and listen to it probably because I couldn't walk on but it was very good.

The other thing I remember was stopping in a pub for a cup of coffee. At this stage, I wasn't allowed alcohol so I had to have a cup of coffee. The Psychologist had said that there was some confusion over stroke victims being allowed alcohol and so they said no-one who had been a victim should be allowed alcohol for about a year. At this stage, I took what they said as gospel and therefore did not attempt to buy alcohol, more amazingly, was the fact that Jacki thought that she should also withdraw from alcohol whilst I was present.

The next week was getting exciting as it was obvious they wanted me out, and make no mistake, I made it clear I wanted to go as well. All the classes were getting more hectic but also less people were involved, and I was getting left alone more and more. Jacki had been working behind the scenes yet again and one evening a Solicitor arrived from London to see if there was any sense to the stroke and, if possible, if action be taken against the hospital. It was fairly brave to have thought of doing this at NHS Amersham Hospital, but Jacki expected me to be there for some time yet, so we booked a private room and waited to see what would happen. I guess she was there for about an hour but it seemed far longer and by the end of her time with us, I was truly exhausted and ready for a long night's sleep.

She went through the events of that night and the next few weeks, which I found a bit distressing because I knew nothing about this, but Jacki was able to tell her what I had been through. She seemed totally shocked by what had happened to me and kept saying they would do all they could do to get some compensation for me. Whilst she was adamant there had been negligence on behalf of the hospital she could not, at this stage, determine whether or not there was any causation to the stroke. I still don't really understand causation in the legal sense but I just had to rely on the Solicitors to prove it. We agreed she seemed to know what she was talking about and we agreed to let them act for us.

Also in this week, I had agreed with the hospital and Jacki that we would have a planning meeting and allocate a team of people to me. I didn't really know what the team was for but they all seemed quite happy with this and Jacki was there to know what the plan was. This was to take place at about one o'clock at NHS Amersham Hospital, but then at about quarter past twelve, they decided I should take the lead and we would go out shopping at Tesco's for some specific items to make sure I was still mentally coherent and could be understood.

I was going to walk at the front and two staff, a Physiotherapist and Occupational Therapist, would follow me from behind and stop if anything became too trying. I was conscious Jacki was coming up shortly and I asked them how I should walk. Do I go at my natural speed or go a bit slower for them? My North Pole speed had gone, but I still walked quickly, although had to stop far more often. They told me to go as I felt best, but given the short time span and, needing to impress them, I went as fast as I could. Walking there and back was difficult, but I knew the way and was able to do it with a surprisingly few number of breaks and I was just late for the one o'clock start.

My power of focus took over and I was determined to achieve this and fast and I did. When we arrived back, I was totally exhausted, but I had achieved the objectives in a manner which had to show I no longer needed to be in hospital.

Unfortunately, it made us aware of something we hadn't been too bothered about, but that was that my brain had been burnt and I had lost some of the thinking power I had before the stroke. The test asked me to get a copy of The Sun which even now I am adamant I did but in fact I bought The Mirror, although the Psychologist laughed this off as saying I was just showing off it did hit home a bit. I wanted to go home so I didn't say anything then. I am also told I had a close shave with a car although my memory of this is that I had plenty of room and had to cross the road as two halves as it was busy. This may have just been a case of my being better placed to make the call or it may have actually been true, either way I have been more careful since.

As if to punish me, Jacki arrived at Tesco's just as I got there. She was going to buy a small amount of stuff there, take it home and then come up to the planning meeting. She saw me and kept calling but I was on a test and could not make contact and just had to keep walking.

Fortunately, I turned to the people behind me and one of them had a word with her so she realised I was not being rude. She has since told me that my eyes were different, she only sees it occasionally but I was determined to achieve the objective.

On the test I did have to stop quite a few times, but I proved that, given the right motivation, I could still just about walk which may appear quite a glib thing to say but this meant a huge amount to me. Jacki and I went down to the planning meeting very pleased with myself, only to find it was postponed for a few minutes while we waited for the Physiotherapist who had walked with me, to have his lunch.

The meeting itself was a short lived affair and, clearly the purpose of it was because they always had a meeting and recorded that they had had a meeting. I was actually quite disappointed with this when I had the time and energy to think about it but at the time it was great because it had clarified they wanted me out as soon as possible. The Physiotherapist who walked with me actually said, albeit as a joke, that from a physiotherapy viewpoint the walk showed I needed it less than him and he played a lot of rugby in his spare time! However, it is worth emphasising I was very tired after a short walk.

The next weekend was coming and I was looking forward to having the weekend off as well, when Jacki turned up and told me that she had a job interview for an Acute Medical Staff Nurse post at NHS Borders General Hospital in Scotland. She would be leaving on Tuesday and coming back on Thursday. I was pleased she had an interview but still didn't really know much about the area, particularly Peebles which is where we would live if she got the job. This would not implicitly stop me having a weekend off which I am afraid at that stage was all that bothered me.

The weekend off was a home weekend and Jacki was allowed to take me home, and fortunately, because I could walk they were not coming to assess my home before such a weekend as that would have delayed it and I would not have been allowed off. This weekend was marvellous because, although Jacki was going away soon, I would be back at NHS Amersham Hospital then and this weekend we just had to be in and around my home. The most exciting part about this was I would get to see my kitten. I say kitten but she was an eleven year old cat. She spent a lot of time outdoors and I still saw her as a kitten.

Just prior to coming for the weekend, we were told that I could leave NHS Amersham Hospital on Tuesday, as long as Jacki was there. We realised this presented a problem as Jacki was leaving for Scotland that day. We spoke to the hospital and they confirmed that Jacki's mother being at our home would be alright and, reluctantly, they agreed to let me go home in a taxi. This meant Jacki had to go to Tunbridge Wells on Monday to fetch her mother to look after me and I was very pleased that she did.

I went back to NHS Amersham Hospital on Monday which was strange, as I didn't want to be there and actually no one wanted me to be there. So I worked my way through the Monday just waiting to go and then Tuesday came. I knew I would have to wait for my blood tests and there results to be determined so they could set me up on the correct Warfarin levels, but then I would be free to go. I left at about eleven o'clock and, it would have been slightly sooner, but when they rang for a taxi they said I would be at the front but I was with the Psychologist at the back of the hospital.

All-in-all I was only in Amersham for just over two weeks which, believe me, is as long as you want to be in a place like that but I was expecting to be there for four weeks at least.

So, I took the taxi back to my then home knowing that Jacki had gone to Scotland for an interview, but at least her mother was there and most importantly Pippy the kitten was there. It was pretty good weather, so I thought I might not see her until this evening. As I opened the door I met Jacki's mother and she suggested I called Pippy. I called her but nothing happened for about five minutes and then she came running inside and sat on my lap for about an hour, purring. As far as Pippy was concerned that is a true welcome back.

13   Life Post Stroke – Chalfont St Peter

I arrived home and it was fantastic to be back in the real world again, only it was a very different real world from the one I had known previously. At this stage, I was still pretending I would go back to work eventually but I think, in reality, I knew then I wouldn't be working again and although she never admitted it Jacki had long since reached this conclusion.

So the first day I just spent at home doing nothing. I slept a bit, pottered around but basically I didn't know what to do. I thought I would just watch television but I couldn't find anything interesting on so I just did nothing which was very easy for me to do. Before my accident I would have to do something even if it was just think, or watch television. Jacki's mother was excellent as she just left me to my own devices but made sure things such as meals were done at sensible times.

The next day I got up wondering what I would do that day, but also knowing that Jacki would be returning at some point. This was perhaps my biggest cause of concern, what would I do each day? This was going to take a long time to resolve and whilst I am much better now than I was there is no doubt I am far worse at this than before the accident.

I decided I would have to get up properly in terms of having a shower and eating breakfast but I wasn't sure what I was letting myself in for. I went to the shower and I got in, but only just. I had to cling on to the window sill as if my life depended on it. I then lifted my right leg over the bath before bringing the left leg in as well. Something which I would have done automatically in a couple of seconds now appeared to take for ever, in reality it was probably about three minutes. Whilst I could stand on them, my legs were both very weak and I was struggling before I had even turned the water on.

I was pleased to see that Jacki had not altered the temperature of the water so I turned it on to its maximum. It came on and it came all over me and it was scalding hot. I didn't know why because I checked Jacki had not changed the temperature; anyway I had to turn the temperature down a little bit and try again. I checked my body and although it had felt like I was being burnt there were no burns on me but it was an interesting shower. I just hoped I hadn't turned it down too much as it would be a pain if Jacki and I required different temperatures. As it happened, whilst Jacki knew it was a bit cooler she could live with it.

I'd managed to avoid all the cooking and drink-making duties yesterday, it hadn't been deliberate, but Jacki's mother had just done them all. I started with the easy task of making us both coffees. Whilst I succeeded, without leaving any obvious error I was amazed at how confusing it all was, and whilst we always put the milk in at the end for some reason I strayed from this and put it in before the water. Not a serious problem, but interesting that it should happen now and enough to put me off the cooking duties for another few days.

Having done the early morning duties I had pretty much had enough for the day. It seems fairly silly to say that even now, but the truth is whilst I can get on and do things the thought and effort involved does take a huge amount out of me. I believed at this time I had about two or three hours of effort a day and the rest of the time I would be sleeping, or just sitting there doing nothing, and I am good at doing nothing now. This has improved a bit over time, but even now I am probably only at four or five hours.

Jacki came home in the late afternoon and it was great to see her and we could be together, although I was not sure how normally we could live but never mind, we were together. Tomorrow was going to be a busy day as we had a Warfarin run at a local health clinic and then we had to take her mother back to Tunbridge Wells. So, although I stayed awake until it was about ten o'clock, I deliberately didn't do very much and just let Jacki and her mother do whatever they wanted. The two of them can chat together about anything for hours and I just left them to it.

The next day I had the same problems with the shower, and I realised that the shower problem would probably exist until we got a walk-in shower. That could only be in our own home somehow. I managed to get the coffee sorted out, which may not sound impressive but I was over the moon with myself because I made the coffee and then added the milk. This meant nothing to the others in the house but I saw this as a real result.

The house was rented and Jacki had told me that when she told the letting agent about my situation hoping they would help us out, they said "oh well, never mind and you may as well leave when your existing contract expires"! Whilst we thought this was unfair, it probably made sense for both parties. From their viewpoint they didn't want us staying there, not earning enough of an income to pay the rent and it gave us the incentive to get up and go. In fact we ended up leaving in August with a November deadline.

Whilst Jacki had told me this when I was in hospital, it was only now that she repeated it that I understood what it actually meant. This was going to be a joint issue for the next couple of months but we had a bit of money in various bank accounts so I was sure we would be able to find a solution, but unlikely in Chalfont St Peter. Why would we choose to live there if I wasn't working at all? Jacki came back from Scotland knowing that she had a part-time job at NHS Borders General Hospital and, whilst it was part-time, it was enough to get started with and so we decided that Scotland, in particular the town of Peebles, was where we should go.

Peebles was chosen because, whilst it was about twenty miles from the hospital and a rather tricky twenty miles, Jacki had some family in Peebles and she knew it although I didn't, but I have moved so often that I was not worried about not knowing an area. The cost of Peebles was relatively high for Scotland but nothing compared to what we had down south and whilst, with hindsight we could have afforded a reasonable living space in Chalfont St Peter, we didn't know it at the time and where we are in Scotland we have a three bedroom bungalow on the edge of woods which is just not possible for the money down south and we have a bit of cash put aside for savings.

So we decided we were going to Peebles in due course and we needed to go up there and find a house. I could only deal with a couple of things a day and it seemed a big issue but it would have to wait because, that day, I had two big problems to sort out. By big, I meant big for me, in fact they are really quite small but it is amazing how every day normal activities become major problems that need thought to resolve.

Jacki took me to the Warfarin centre, it was just a Health Clinic but I called it the Warfarin centre and we knew what I meant. The problem had got marginally better, but at the time I got very confused about words and in particular names. This was a lot easier than I thought. We sat down and waited for our name to be called. Sitting down was harder than I thought as everyone else there was significantly older than me, and I think they believed I was helping other people. The chairs all ran out for people to sit down and one old person who must have had something wrong with him to be given Warfarin came up to me, missing about ten people his age and asked me if I could move to which I just stared at him. Fortunately, I was called then and I did move for the Nurse, but not for the old man, who realised I was attending for myself did look embarrassed and did apologise, I think, as it was muffled.

Once we had been to the Health Centre that was one problem dealt with and the problem was that my sense of direction was now useless and I needed help going anywhere new now, even if like this it was at the back of somewhere I went to regularly. Once I had been, I could usually get back there, but would probably still need a map or at least a set of directions, but that problem was dealt with for now. I would need to go the Health Centre twice a week for a couple of weeks and then weekly as long as I was on Warfarin.

Fortunately, Jacki would take me every time because I could not drive and, whilst I would have thought of this as a nice walk to the top of the High Street and right a bit before the stroke, now it would probably kill me. I would have been happy trying because one of the biggest things I had to deal with was knowing what I could no longer do. Based on my previous life this journey would have been nothing and at this stage I didn't know any better but Jacki did. Whereas, in the past, I would just have gone and probably on foot Jacki knew better although I did not, so Jacki booked to come on all visits. At the time I didn't recognise why, but now I do.

The second problem for me was actually a trip in the car but it felt so dramatic. We were going to take her mother home. Due to my crash I had no driving licence at this point and it was our car so I am afraid Jacki had to drive both ways. Driving-wise, this is not a problem, as she would usually have expected to drive anyway but it was nice knowing that if Jacki started getting tired I could take over, but never mind. Even so, sitting in the car and having a full pit-stop in Tunbridge Wells really did take it out of me. Historically I would just have fallen asleep in the car but now I couldn't. Jacki kept telling me just to sleep but I stayed awake albeit only just all the time we were travelling in the car.

I was awake, but I didn't really know what was going on, which led me to realise another couple of problems I had. Firstly, I didn't know whether or not I could do what had been simple things. Currently I was still going with 'yes, I could do them' particularly if walking was involved but I usually regretted it. The other thing I realised was that things were going on around me, but I knew nothing about them, whereas a couple of months ago I was involved and aware of all of the problems. I reckon that I was probably asleep at least fourteen hours of every day but sleeping wasn't so much of a problem. The problem here was that, whilst I was awake, there were only about one or two hours that I was alert. This has got better, but I am still only truly awake and something bordering on alert about three or four hours a day. I can do five or six one day but I will be virtually useless the next day.

I was very much of the point of view of living for today, and that means every problem was an issue only if I was actively doing something about it. If I was not, it was forgotten until I had to deal with it. Whilst this was a problem of sorts, and who knows what I would have done with something very big, it made me living my life exceptionally simply although I am afraid it drove Jacki mad.

On our return home, I noticed that we seemed to have acquired a lot of clothes that needed ironing. Before the stroke, I would have done these easily in about an hour and I didn't really think anything of it, so I decided I would do them the following day. The morning came and I began the ironing and it took absolutely ages, I had spent an hour on ironing shirts and I was barely a quarter through, and I was incredibly exhausted. I didn't know what it was, ironing may be boring but there is not a technical issue to it, but all clothes have a bit of weight, as does the iron which, together with using an iron and not burning yourself, uses a surprising amount of concentration and this exhausts me even today.

The exhaustion from the ironing was no doubt increased by my brain not having seen that particular set of issues before. In the past, the first time I had ironed I would have known what to do, but now I have to work everything out again. I obviously still knew the basics of ironing but I didn't know how to fold the clothes so that no creases occurred and perhaps the most frightening aspect of this was that holding a set of clothes was hard work. I was exhausted at the simplest aspect of ironing and this really shocked me although Jacki, once again, had determined this.

Jacki had decided that we should go out for a meal one day to celebrate my being back in the real world. I agreed to this, in fact I was strangely excited, but I felt we had to make it lunch time rather than an evening meal. She was more than happy to make it a lunchtime meal, in fact that has become a bit of a habit of ours now. Lunch really had two advantages, one it was sufficiently early in the day that I was unlikely to become exhausted and two, it was quieter. We decided to go to a small Italian restaurant near where we lived and used to go fairly often before.

We met the waiter and told him about my situation which explained why we hadn't been for a few months and also explained the change in the shape of my face to him. We decided to order and I had to scan the options closely for a suitable choice. Normally, I would have had steak there but given my fractured jaws from the crash that was especially banned so I had to choose something else. I decided to be traditional and choose a simple Italian dish so I chose spaghetti. Jacki asked my permission, as she does, but there was no way I would stop her having what she wanted just because I couldn't, so she had steak and accompanied it with a glass of red wine for the first time in months. Because the Psychologist at NHS Amersham Hospital had told me I couldn't have alcohol for a year, I just had water. When the dishes arrived mine looked nice but Jacki's looked delicious. My dish was chosen because I thought it would be simple to eat as it was just spaghetti and, providing I cut my pasta up, it should be relatively easy. I still don't really know why, but it was really difficult. I presume it was because it is relatively soft but it just dripped and I spent the entire meal wiping my face. As I said, fortunately we knew the waiter and quite liked him and he brought us several tissues to keep wiping my face with. Having said that, the food itself was gorgeous and I was glad we had gone. Going in the afternoon proved to be a good idea as the waiter had time to look after us and there wasn't anyone else near us.

I think the reason Jacki took me out for lunch was that she was getting fed up with me insisting on helping with dinner and then getting badly burnt as a result. I got burned a few times in this session but perhaps the most notable was one day when I was serving up and left a very hot dish sitting on my arm for what seemed like minutes but I just didn't have the strength to move it. I got a very bad burn mark on the inside of my arm just below the elbow. After that, we realised I was best left away from cooking although the main problem actually arose in serving up meals rather than in cooking them. I have no sense of sequencing even now so following cooking instructions requires us to be very brave.

One of the problems of eating pureed food which I had to for a long period of time is that it tastes bearable but nothing more than that, but obviously it has a lot of water in it. As a result, I had lost a lot of weight and, as I mentioned before, I didn't have much spare weight to lose. Whilst I was at NHS Amersham Hospital, I weighed myself on their proper weights and I was only forty three kilograms and really I needed to be at least fifty, ideally fifty five kilograms. I was prescribed supplement drinks to increase my weight whilst I was at NHS Amersham Hospital, but some extra help was required whilst I was out so our doctor made an urgent referral to a Dietician.

The Dietician was incredible and, had I been thinking normally, I would have been scared stiff as Jacki was. I couldn't think so fast, so I thought she had just seen a problem and it was only later I realised the extent of it. She was convinced I had become malnourished and would struggle to stay alive. To this day, I do not know if she just panicked at seeing me or whether she was actually right but it scared us, although it took a bit longer to scare me than it did Jacki. Jacki had not known my hospital discharge weight. As a result of seeing her, I had a vast schedule of drinks to take during the day and a list of instructions on how to fortify my daily meal regime and it started immediately. Plus we had to get a serious concoction of vitamins which I still take every day.

I wasn't too bothered about the meal fortifications as I often would have done if I had got the stuff and, all this meant was, I had the excuse to buy the stuff. I did drink black coffee before the stroke but in hospital it didn't taste very nice, so I put milk in it anyway and I sort of got used to this. Now, I had to have milk in my coffee but again this was not too challenging and, in fact, now I almost always have it white as I am now more used to white.

The real problem with the regime was the extra containers of drink. Each bottle was meant to be about six hundred calories and I was meant to take two a day in addition to my, now fortified, meals. This was extremely difficult and, in a way, one of the upsides of moving to Peebles is that I had increased my weight by the time I went so the Dietician didn't have such a traumatic start and dealt with me accordingly. I did manage the drinks, only just, but the truth is it impacted on the other meals I was eating. Still, never mind. Having this tough new regime did mean I managed to put the initial weight desired on reasonably quickly.

This period of time seems quite confusing as really all I had to do was occasional medical things but I felt that I had no personal time at all and, the reason for this, was that I had to concentrate on the medical things when I went to them and that I am afraid meant I couldn't really do anything else all day.

One further medical side I had to deal with was that of occupational testing. I had done the basic work inside the hospitals but it had to keep going. As a result, I went to the local Health Clinic with Jacki and waited for the occupational testing people to meet with me. They were surprisingly late which always makes Jacki mad before the first meeting began, and it didn't get much better when it did finally begin.

The truth is, they didn't really know what to do with me, they were quite comfortable with a serious injury and dealing with major changes but they didn't know how to get me doing more of the complex things. They gave me a few quizzes and crosswords which were alright but I had already shown I could understand the language and, whilst vocabulary is important, it is not everything and they could not cope with the numeracy dropping. Unfortunately, as a Chartered Accountant, it is the numeracy I was most interested in.

I went to these people four times, but I was getting a bit annoyed about it. I decided to keep going until, I left or they didn't want to see me. I was getting annoyed but they mentioned some free software which would be available to me and should be of use. The Occupational Therapist had the software just before I left for Peebles and so she decided to come on the way home from work one day. She came and downloaded the software on my computer but unfortunately could not begin the software until I paid the initial royalty fee. She was going to get this paid by a charity but obviously this needed to be agreed at the next charity meeting which was about a month away and, by then, I would have left the region. We weren't really sure about what would happen with this but it actually got solved very easily in Peebles. As the software was written by the medical staff in Peebles itself, anyone with a Peebles postcode got it free.

I had a couple of visits to a head doctor in Chesham. I say head doctor as that was a simple definition I used at the time but obviously he was a qualified Neurologist and, with that, he was also very specialist in terms of strokes. It was quite a distance for us to travel to the doctors and we didn't know where we were going so we left very early and then found the centre with ease so we arrived there about an hour before we needed to. We decided we may as well go in and wait for the meeting which we did. We announced we were here very early but we could wait until it was due. We started waiting but after quarter of an hour the doctor said he had some spare time so would we like to start, which of course we did.

This was an amazing meeting, not only did we start forty five minutes early but we used the hour the meeting was booked for and finished pretty much dead on time. He went through everything and gave me a lot of useful little things to do. Until now, the medical side was only concerned with keeping me alive and didn't bother too much about making things easy for me. He made sure that everything he talked about was understood by me and if he could make any suggestions he did.

The most notable thing he said was about drinking alcohol. He asked me if I had had a drink since the accident and I said no because the Psychologist had told me not to so I was not drinking. He said "don't worry about that" and whilst I shouldn't get drunk there was no reason I shouldn't have a drink. The result of this instruction was obvious and we bought a bottle of wine on the way home and I had a drink that night. One bottle was more than enough, the drink was fantastic but I could only manage one glass, and it stayed like that for a reasonable length of time, but at least Jacki was able to share a drink with me.

There was one task with Peebles that needed completing before we moved there for good and that was to find a house. It was going to be quite difficult, not actually finding a house, but how we were going to pay for it. Historically, I had been the biggest earner but now I had effectively retired and was left to state benefits instead of earnings. We would have enough money to purchase the house outright, but had not expected this, so a lot of money was put aside until the following April and we didn't know about the critical illness insurance at that point in time. The good news was that Jacki knew people in Peebles and they had agreed to take a look around for us.

We decided the best thing to do was to go up to Peebles for a few days and agree to look around a few houses. We would probably have to rent to start with, which annoyed me a bit because the accident has destroyed my sense of adventure. Prior to the stroke, I would happily have rented and moved around but now I just wanted a house of my own where I could possibly stay forever. Jacki is a bit of a nomad at heart but I think she has accepted the house is the way it is for me.

We were invited to stay with a relative of Jacki's for a few days and we went up to Peebles. We could only manage three days because of our dealings with the Warfarin clinic and a few other constraints we had, but three days was a start. Unbeknown to me, Jacki was well ahead of me in terms of finding a house and had spent a lot of time whilst I'd been asleep looking at Peebles properties for rent and for sale on the internet and had found one that we would go and look around. In fact, Jacki had already got her relative to have a look around the property for us and had rung Jacki up from the sun room of the property to suggest that, whilst it needed updating, we should see it. We asked whether it was for rent or sale and, unbelievably this property felt right for us, in that it had been for sale only but now it was for rent or for sale.

Our first day in Peebles we had booked a meeting at the house which was a great success. It was a bungalow which was rare in Peebles and now I had no choice and needed to live in a bungalow. I could barely make it up or down the stairs in a house and I knew I would find it near impossible so I had decided on a bungalow.

I also noticed that I could walk in and out of town from there, the gradient was pretty much neutral, the distance was not too bad and there were plenty of seats along the way. This meant a huge amount to me as I don't believe my walking is going to get any better and I still am a keen walker, I just can't do it as well as I would like to. The big problems to me whilst I am walking are gradient changes and that's whether or not I am going up or downhill and of course, the distance, particularly without stops.

Finally the great thing about the bungalow was it was located in a cul-de-sac and more importantly it is near the end of the cul-de-sac. Its' view at the front is of a house but mostly of a well-structured garden but the real advantage is its view at the rear. We have a view over a small piece of woodland rising up the hill where we can just see some other houses at the top. This hill is very steep which may sound bad given my condition but it also has the great advantage that building there would be ridiculously expensive and so we were fairly confident we would be left with a private woodland behind.

All the great things about the house were to do with the location of it, the inside of the house has enough rooms, but it was fair to say they had been neglected over time. As I said, it had enough room, so whilst we would need to improve it internally, we could easily manage to live there when it was being done. Given our plan was to move once and forever, but we didn't have all the money ready at that point, meant we had to be quite clever about buying the house and about gradually doing it up once we owned it.

I had had a stroke and that resulted in me being severely cognitively impaired, so it may have taken a bit longer than it would have done prior to the stroke, but we decided we could make an offer to rent the property until the end of April at which point we would buy the property. We knew we would have sufficient reserves to purchase the property at the end of April as the savings in a fixed interest and fixed withdrawal date would become available to us in April. From the vendor's viewpoint, he had a fixed income for the next eight months, then an agreement to sell the property. One advantage of buying in Scotland is that when the missives are done it is contractually binding and so both parties knew the rent and the sale would happen.

Having looked around the house and deciding on an offer, we needed to get some Solicitors to act for us. This was actually quite difficult in Peebles because there are not too many obvious Solicitors and, at that stage, we only knew of one and unfortunately they were acting for the seller. They argued they were able to use certain rural rules and, providing we were a family member of an existing client, we would be able to use them. Foolishly, we agreed to using them rather than finding an alternative Solicitor.

We went straight to the Solicitors and put in an offer which was accepted, in principle, in the fact that he would rent the property with an agreed sale on a particular date but he wouldn't accept the first price we offered. The failure to accept the first price surprised us a little bit as it had been on the market for a long time, but we offered a second price which, ultimately, was accepted the following day. One good thing about us getting a property, subject to missives, was that we now had some free time, albeit limited, to get to know Peebles.

Getting to know Peebles isn't that difficult because it isn't that big but an afternoon exploring the town was great for getting a good understanding of it. The important thing for me that made me so comfortable in coming up is that, whilst there are hills surrounding Peebles, it itself is relatively flat and self-contained so I could get more or less anything done although I would need to go further out for some specialist items, including hospitals as we only had a small, rural hospital in town.

Whilst we were there, we thought we should go to Jacki's place of work which was near Melrose, about twenty miles away. The distance was not too bad and, unfortunately we went in the middle of the day and it was summer, so we didn't get a feel of the road in the early morning or late at night which would be when Jacki was leaving or returning from work. We had checked with her relatives what they thought and they were happy that Peebles to NHS Borders General Hospital was a perfectly simple trip and would not cause any issues. On the basis of this, when the Solicitor rang whilst we were heading to the hospital and said our first offer was not enough, we pulled into a siding and simply looked at each other and nodded, at which point Jacki gave the second and ultimately accepted price.

Having bought the house we continued on our way to the hospital where we found a place to park, but for me with my new Blue Badge! We didn't realise how difficult Jacki would find parking for work, but then again she would always be early so perhaps there might be a shortage of spaces, but there would always be one available for her. We then did a quick tour around the hospital to see the areas where Jacki would be working but there was a limit to what she could show me without actually being on duty. None the less, we left the hospital immensely satisfied that we had acquired the house and happy that Jacki had a reasonable job to go to.

We left Peebles, happy in the knowledge that we would be back again for good in the near future and what we had to do now was get the rental property ready for giving back to the letting agent and move up north. I was able to do a bit of packing, but after a couple of boxes a day, I had had enough. Providing I did a bit every day, we would be alright, but of course that still left Jacki doing the bulk of the work.

Having decided on Peebles, I realised I needed to see my parents before I went up to Scotland and so I arranged for them to come to Amersham, which was near me, but also on the train for them. Jacki was still immensely disappointed with the way they were with me in hospital and hence she had decided she would not meet up with them. Jacki did, however, agree to take me to Amersham station and pick me up from there when I rang her later in the day. We were blessed in that it was a lovely day and we could look around Amersham rather than just run from venue to venue.

This was a fantastic day in that I was able to speak freely to my parents and show them bits of the area I lived in but also quite an education for me in that my father was showing signs of decline. Being on an away-trip where he didn't know the area was difficult for him and his walking was a real surprise to me. I know I was on good form that day as I had taken things very lightly for a couple of days but even I, albeit, only just managed to out walk him.

As my dad was struggling a bit and they needed to get back to Brighton, I left them at the station in the late afternoon and called Jacki to fetch me. It was a shame knowing I would be going so far from them but also my move had to happen. I only hoped I would be able to see them both again at some stage in the future. I felt I had done the family duty and I still had some counselling to deal with and then I would be ready to move.

The counselling had been happening once a week for a few weeks and we still had a couple left. The Councillor was provided by an accounting charity and her purpose was to try and make us happy that we could fend for ourselves. The woman was fantastic because she just listened and asked us all the right questions, but above all, because she treated Jacki as much of a victim as she treated me. This may sound odd, given that it was me who had had the stroke, but it was Jacki who had to give everything up to care for me. It seemed like the Councillor was the only person who grasped this, she probably wasn't, but it felt that way.

Realising that Jacki was as affected by this as I was; she made sure we were equally tested by the sessions. In fact, I remember feeling a little bit out of one session as she seemed to be concentrating on Jacki a lot more than me. She probably was, because I knew I was the victim, I can do nothing about that, but Jacki had a choice of whether to continue being a victim or not. Quite remarkably, Jacki has still chosen to persevere with me and hence be a victim of the event as well.

The Councillor had a maximum of six sessions with us available to her and she definitely wanted to use them all. The sixth one was due to occur after we had left but she was determined to fit the sixth session in. Ultimately, she found out we had to see the landlords' agent at three o'clock on the day we left so she would come around at one o'clock. We told her we would have no belongings in the house as they would already be on their way north but she had no problem with that.

The day before the Councillor came, the removal men were in to clear out the Chalfont St Peter home and move it up to Peebles. We have moved several times, but the actual move itself is hard work and you do need to keep your mind in what you are doing. Fortunately, Jacki was wide awake because I got very tired very quickly. It got so bad that at one point I had to go outside and sleep in the car for a bit. In doors was no longer possible to sleep as they had someone in each room and the bedding had gone. The car didn't really work as it was too hot that day and the sun piercing through the windscreen was too hot, even for a cold creature like me. Jacki got a bit upset about this and luckily one of the removal men saw us and came up with an idea. He suggested that we delay storing a particular mattress and I could sleep on that, providing we placed it somewhere in the garden. Knowing I would not need to sleep for too long I had no hesitation in accepting. I was probably there for about forty minutes and it was wonderful to have a sleep during the day. When I awoke, I was replenished and quite happily continued moving.

The sixth and final session was a strange affair in that we were excited about moving but didn't really know what we were going to do when we did get there. The Councillor was very sensible on this occasion and, whilst she did let us wander off about moving to Peebles, she also made us remember that we were going to Peebles as a part-time Nurse and full-time care-supported individual. I was not going as a Chartered Accountant who could really get work anytime, at least if he was not too fussy. This did register with us; it was a different move from before. We had to get this right as we couldn't keep moving as we had done previously. She left and the last thing we had to do was to meet the landlord's agent to hand the property back. The landlord had had a string of people come to the house over the last couple of months to consider renting the property but had found one a couple of weeks ago. Just before the agent came to inspect the house, there was a person putting up a new 'to let' sign on the house. This was a little bit odd, so I went to speak to the guy and he said the rental had fallen through. We must admit that we were a little bit pleased about this. It seems naughty to say that but, we hadn't been treated fantastically by the landlord and now it appeared they were going to lose some rent. We had done our bit so they couldn't blame us at all.

The same person who inspected the house when we arrived was responsible when we left. I was quite pleased about that as he seemed reasonable then. Although it is a lot easier to be reasonable when people are moving in than out, I felt we had a good starting point. As it turned out, Jacki had made sure the building was spotless and he had no problem in agreeing that they should give us back our full deposit. He couldn't say we would get our deposit back or not because that was up to the landlord but, given he thought we should, we knew we would argue with the landlord if necessary. In the end, it turned out not to be a problem and the deposit was fully repaid and early which was fantastic. At that time, the deposit was hard cash and we didn't know how much more we would get so every penny was useful.

Taking the drive up to Peebles was going to be tough for me. Ideally, we would have left first thing in the morning and then taken most of the day to get up there, but the landlords' agent only left at about half past three in the afternoon and we immediately went north, but it was a lot later than we would have liked. Of course, I say it was going to be bad for me, but at this point I still couldn't drive so Jacki had the unenviable task of driving up there.

Her mother had gone up earlier in the week to collect the goods from the removal company and was staying with her brother up there so we knew that, whenever we arrived, the removal van would have been and gone. Before the stroke, I would have been fine and probably just slept as much as I could. That may appear a bit unfair to Jacki, me sleeping next to her in the car, but Jacki was fine with it. Now, although I was feeling very tired, I could no longer ever sleep in cars. I suspect that, having had a crash which has ruined me, I was just too scared to try and sleep. Having said that, I did appear to be managing to get to sleep, but unfortunately a lorry going the other way beeped a fellow lorry and it made me jump up again fearing another crash. That was the only time in the entire trip I almost fell asleep.

We arrived at the house in Peebles at about one o'clock in the morning and just got in and went to sleep. Later that day, we woke up properly and decided to gradually work out what was going where, but there was no urgency for this. It was strange to have moved to a brand new place just after having such a major issue as a stroke but we had no choice and had to look forward to a future in Peebles. The first thing that we had to do was to get the formalities out of the way and ensure that the relevant local doctor's surgery knew of me because I was still going to be undergoing a lot of medical treatment.

This was strange for me; I had moved several times before and never really bothered about registering with medical places so urgently before. I would ring to register for council tax but that would be about it. I used the term council tax because that is what it is but it used to be the poll tax and that is what I mistakenly but repeatedly call it.

We had given the doctor's surgery a bit of warning the last time we were up that we would be coming and would probably expect quite a bit of help from them, but now we had to tell them I'd arrived. Jacki knew Peebles reasonably well because she had been before and it is relatively small so she took us to the local hospital. The local hospital holds pretty much everything that is a basic medical function. It was also where the local stroke service met, so we knew I'd be there a lot, at least to start with, but today we booked an appointment with my doctor so he could get to know the problems with me. One of Jacki's relatives is also disabled and she had given us advice on this and we chose the doctor she had. When we met him, it became apparent why she had suggested him, as there was no doubt that he is on the side of his patients.

As well as making sure the formal links were made, we wanted to make sure that the informal links were made, as, although I was ill I would be up in Peebles a long time. Before we came I had checked whether or not Peebles had a Round Table and I was a bit surprised, but it did. Through the Round Table website we contacted them and told them what had happened and, also, that I was shortly going to be kicked out of Table because of my age, but that I was coming to Peebles and if I could get to meet them that would be fantastic.

To my surprise they responded pretty much straight away. I was surprised that they responded to the website quickly, because they are just ordinary people who do Round Table in an evening as something to do. They told me that there was the Chairman's barbecue, an annual event in a couple of weeks' time and that this also included partners. This was fantastic news for us as it meant we could meet the Tablers and their partners as soon as possible.

Saturday came and we knew that in the afternoon we would go to the barbecue, so I decided I would do nothing beforehand, because I wanted to be able to concentrate as much as possible on the event. It was at the Chairman's house at the other end of town so we drove, although Peebles is not that big, I felt better being driven than I did completing a walk. I would not have thought about this a year ago, but now it would be quite an expedition. This was a bit unfair on Jacki because she would be limited in the amount she could drink but she just smiled and drove.

When we arrived at the event, it was superb because I think everyone had been told I was ill and that I was new to the area and they seemed to be making an effort to talk to me. Over the course of the afternoon I spoke to most of the Tablers and had a relatively in-depth chat to them. As well as this, Jacki got on well with the partners which had been a concern of mine, as I knew I would get on all right with the Tablers as there was a reason we all shared in joining Table, but I didn't know about Jacki.

We stayed there for a couple of hours, but by then I was struggling. Although they were all well behaved and respectful that I was ill, I needed to concentrate on all of them and, the way the stroke has burnt my brain, this meant making a huge amount of effort. The other thing which I was beginning to notice was how cold I always felt. To start with, we just put it down to being in Scotland and Scotland is a lot colder than the south of England and definitely than South Africa. It wasn't a scorching hot day, but I was cold and I was the only person who felt truly cold, or at least admitted to it. The most worrying part was that included Jacki and, before the stroke, I had always felt a little bit warmer than her.

I got home and started to warm up and so I forgot I had been cold, but it was becoming an issue. At the time I just thought Jacki had a thing about me wearing my slippers but if I went anywhere from the bedroom at night I would always insist on wearing slippers. Again, I hadn't thought why this would be, I was cold and I needed to keep my feet warm so I would put my slippers on. Of course, because the stroke had happened recently, it would take about ten minutes to put both slippers on. Now I can do it in about two minutes, which I still find amazing as, pre-stroke, I would have died if I was told it will take two minutes to put on two slippers!

Of course, leaving bed usually occurred at night which, if I was Jacki, would really have annoyed me. All she wanted to do was to sleep and I would take about half an hour doing a simple thing like go to the toilet. As I said, it would have annoyed me and it did annoy Jacki, but even now I have to do it although now I have reduced the time dramatically. I believe it is because it is cold on my feet when I walk anywhere bare-footed and so I have to put the slippers on. Jacki believes it is because I was so conditioned to wearing shoes when in hospital and I haven't grown out of it yet.

Connected with this is the chore of getting up in the morning, and I do mean chore. Before the stroke, I simply had a shower and then got dressed. All of a sudden, this had become a serious engagement and, instead of taking a few minutes, it was now probably an hour long and even longer if I had to undergo the torture that shaving had now become. I don't know if shaving had become so painful because of the stroke or because I broke my jaws in five places in the crash. Either way, it still hurts now when I shave and then it was even worse.

Getting up is a nightmare part of the day for me and mainly because, on the face of it, I can't see anything wrong with it but I fear it every day. The first thing is to decide what to wear and I didn't have this problem in hospital as Jacki brought me clothes in and if I wore them slightly crooked no one would mind. In fact, being in hospital I doubt they would notice. The main difficulty is of course warmth, I have to be warm and again this wasn't a problem in hospital and I was in Chalfont St Peter during the summer so didn't realise I had a problem until we lived in Peebles. Now I am very aware I have a problem. We have spoken to a few doctors about this and they have confirmed that I have broken a link of my internal radiator and, unfortunately, that is that and I will now always be a few degrees colder than everyone else is.

The first thing with getting dressed is I have to decide on the basics of pants and socks. Pants are all right but socks are a different story. I have bought several thick woollen socks since I have been up in Peebles because I get very cold now, even in the summer I usually wear a pair of these or my old walking socks. It does upset me a bit, because I know the reason I am wearing these is because I am cold, rather than because it is cold. Anyway, it doesn't really matter, I am colder than I should be and so I wear bigger and extra clothes.

Once I have decided on the socks I have my biggest choice of the day, do I want full, half or no thermals? I had a couple of pairs for the North Pole trip and I virtually hadn't used them since, but now they were constantly in the wash and so I had to buy several more pairs of thermal clothes. The ones I bought are not quite as good so the choice has effectively doubled and must be made daily. These two choices of socks and thermals are a decision that is needed every day and it needs to be right, although I have finally learnt to be on the cautious side. If there is any doubt at all, I wear the thickest set that I am comfortable with.

Historically, I would wear the thinnest set I was comfortable with because, if I was wrong I might start sweating and feeling uncomfortable, but now I know that it is very, very unlikely. In fact, I had decided I would tell my doctor I don't sweat anymore but then a few times I have been sweating uncontrollably. I mentioned this to my doctor at a session and he said that because the stroke effectively damaging my internal radiator, I would, on most occasions, feel cold. That would be a normal day, but there would be situations where it realised it had broken and then heated up too fast, hence my sweating sessions.

Fortunately I have only had a few sweating sessions. He mentioned mine was the normal way, but it is possible it is the other way around with sweating sessions being the norm and occasional coldness. In fact, he knows of one woman whom half of her gets cold and the other half hot at the same time. I think, with hindsight, I will accept my way because the other ways are terrible. We probably wouldn't have come to Scotland if I knew this would be a problem though.

Having decided on what clothes to wear, I then have to put them on. I can put them on but it is difficult and Jacki will always check I have put them on properly. Buttons on shirts and particularly the sleeves can be a real problem. My hands are reasonably articulate, at least so I want to believe, but in truth they are not that good and I regularly end up in a mess. It is amazing how many stupid things can be done with buttons. You can leave them thinking they are done up when they are only half done up or not at all, or the worst thing is that you have put one button up to the wrong hole.

It is not just buttons that present a problem; it is every item of clothing. I should be able to tell, but it is amazing how often Jacki grabs my jumper and pulls it down so I am wearing it normally rather than having it caught on my shirt. It annoys me having to have Jacki check what should be easily spotted by anyone of any age, however, I don't spot it. It is very embarrassing but fortunately Jacki will spot it and, whilst it is distressing being so reliable on one person, it needn't be known by others. It can be very important that Jacki is around.

Even then the event is not over. If we decide to go out, there are further questions around the possibility of wearing gloves, a scarf and possibly a hat as well. Just deciding we will walk about half a mile down by the river is quite an event. It has to be very hot for me not to wear gloves. My hands get cold if outside and because I have to have a walking stick I can't warm my hands up in the pockets very easily so I tend to wear gloves and I have four pairs of different thickness so I can wear the appropriate ones for the weather.

The hat and scarf is more of a decision if it is winter, although I am amazed at how much of the year this is. Scotland wasn't the best place to choose with this temperature, now that we know, but even so it amazes me how late in the year I stop wearing hats and scarves or indeed how early I start wearing them. I probably don't wear them from mid-May to mid-September so about four months, whereas pre-stroke on an admittedly warmer climate I would only wear a hat and scarf on very special occasions.

Having decided what to wear, I always have the traumatic question of do I shave or not. I used to quite enjoy shaving as I would do it every day while I was showering and it was a fairly nice relaxing way of getting up, now I hate it and I do mean hate it. Originally, with my jaws having broken in five places, they have remoulded themselves pretty well, but I still have braces on my teeth, elastic bands in three places between top and bottom jaws and a permanent metal plate inside my mouth. I could probably accept that, but because of my stroke I have a distorted sense of touch which means I am permanently in danger of hurting myself whenever I shave. I tell myself that I won't hurt myself too much because I would feel it very quickly but it does scare me.

It is quite frightening that I had a special stick from years ago, that I could use if I got a shaving cut, and it was virtually unused. Now that I have had the stroke, this stick gets used more often than not. In fact, I am very proud of myself when I finish shaving without bleeding and therefore don't need the stick. I get the stick out every time I shave which I never did before because it was so occasional when it would happen.

I know I am being silly and I should just get an electric shaver because I would be less likely to cut myself but I don't want to. It is do with me not really wanting to admit that I have had a stroke and I would rather still shave manually and risk cutting myself badly than buy an electric razor. This was how I spoke about shaving to myself but now Jacki has been proved right and I have acquired an electric razor. Jacki mentioned this to me on a few occasions, but one day I had almost pulled my facial skin off and at that point we decided an electric razor was a good buy. I don't shave anywhere near as closely as I used to with a blade but at least I haven't cut myself since.

The very first person who came to see us at our house in Peebles was a service organiser of Chest Heart and Stroke Scotland, so I always have a sense of loyalty to her. She came one morning to see how I was and whether or not I would like to go to their stroke meetings every Wednesday. Obviously, I agreed to go, despite her warning me that most people there were very old, but I was in the stroke group now and they are generally old people. The information she had about strokes was very interesting, but even more important was the fact she knew a lot of people who had had a stroke.

The most interesting stroke victim around Peebles was a young woman whom, apparently had been in her mid-thirties and pregnant at the time, when she had a stroke. It seems unfair of me, but this got my attention because it was the first person I had heard of who was younger than me and had a stroke. I thought thank God for that, someone younger than me has experienced this too. Her stroke was about seven years ago and it seemed to have been a slightly lessor stroke than mine, but she now knows what to do when problems start occurring. At this point in time, I didn't even know I was having problems; let alone how to sort them. Even now I can be unsure about this.

This young woman wasn't at the first meeting because she only goes every month or so but she was there the second time and I was very glad when she sat next to me so we could talk. The first hour or so of the meeting was to talk around the table about anything. Usually it had a stroke connection but it didn't matter, it was just for us to improve our speech as much as possible.

The one thing I realised about this was that apart from this young woman, the next youngest were mid-fifties, but most were probably around seventy. Whilst I wasn't worried about the age, it did make a nice change to be talking about the stroke with a victim who was younger than me.

I kept going for a few months because it did make me focus on the problems I now faced and also, although they were older than me, it was quite comforting to see that I was dealing with my problems quicker than they were. I needed to go to the group meetings when I was first invited as it gave me a proper sense of what had happened to me and they did try to address it as much as possible although, after a while, I just felt too young for the meeting and because of their age the recreational aspects of the meeting were all aimed at older people.

So eventually I left the meetings and had to ring the service organiser up to tell her. It was this phone call that made me realise just how much loyalty I had to her. I really didn't want to tell her, when, in reality it is what happens. Of course she just accepted it, especially as I was going to become a volunteer of what I call CHSS, Chest Heart and Stroke Scotland, but I was still terrified of telling her.

We had been up in Peebles a few months and we knew that shortly the critical illness insurance payment would either be paid or we had lost out due to a technicality. Reading the payment terms it said it would pay out on a stroke but then it also said that if it had been caused by an artery being affected by trauma it would not pay out. We didn't know what had caused my stroke but an artery had been damaged so we just had to wait and see.

I was told my case was being considered by the board on a particular date and, not surprisingly, I heard nothing then so I plucked up the courage and rang them the next day. I seemed to have spent ages getting past all their security requests but I imagine that's because I just wanted to know if they had paid or not. Eventually, I finished all the security requests and the person at the other end said, incredibly calmly, there is a cheque on the way. I wasn't quite as calm as her in my receipt of this news and asked her to confirm the amount coming to me and when.

This was fantastic news. Because it was critical illness cover and expensive, I could only afford a set amount but it was coming and in full, backdated to an amount from when I had the stroke. Although it was fantastic news, both Jacki and I were also a little bit upset. Until now, the stroke was a horrible accident but we sort of lived behind the fact that I could go to work if the situation arose, but now it appeared that at least these people thought it was over. Jacki actually burst into tears which I've seen a few times since my stroke, but never to this degree.

The pay-out meant that, not only could we buy the house when it became due, but because we would have had that amount anyway we could actually put some away for savings which I was desperately going to need. It wasn't the great retirement fund I had been hoping to develop but it would do. The other reason it was fantastic is that Jacki had actually told me about a month before the accident that I wasn't susceptible to these sorts of events and that I should cancel it. I may have taken notice of her, but at that point I was too busy and just kept paying.

For the first few months I received language training from a Speech and Language Therapist. It is nothing personal, because I thought she was great, but I was a little bit disappointed that people thought it was necessary to train me on the English language. I do, however, admit that my use of vocabulary is chosen from a lot narrower pool than before the stroke, and I still have an awful problem with names. There is no doubt I needed to undergo some sort of revision course of language skills but nonetheless, I was still a bit disappointed.

However, the Speech and Language Therapist was a good introduction to Peebles life. She had lived here all her life but was not afraid of other places; in fact she went to London on holiday whilst she was seeing us. This made the sessions doubly useful as we needed to get to know and understand the way of life in Peebles. Although the sessions were just with me, she came to our house and so Jacki would have an opportunity to ask her any questions that we may have about Peebles.

Whilst she was here she had a trainee appointed to her, and she too came. After the first week this girl was asked to prepare and present the sessions, which I guess was quite normal, but it made me laugh because she had obviously taken note in the house and listened to conversation in the first session. She had prepared a customised session covering the North Pole and English rugby but didn't really understand either! As a result, she produced a perfectly good session but I spent longer working out what she meant than I actually did in using the language.

The Speech and Language Therapist was really quite good and, although I didn't like the message that I needed to be taught language skills, I did. In a way I kind of miss the sessions because it was a link to Peebles. I've bumped into her since a couple of times after the end of the sessions, at NHS Hay Lodge Hospital, our local hospital. I'm there for a variety of medical reasons and, officially, that is where she works although often she is out and about. It does make me laugh as she always said, at the end of the sessions; she would get back in touch and see how I am. I met her at NHS Hay Lodge Hospital car park once, so she said please can we do it now. There's no reason not to, so of course I let her but I can't imagine in my job if I'd be allowed to call a quick chat in a car park a catch up!

Jacki was travelling to and from NHS Borders General Hospital for work at least twice and usually three times a week. It became apparent that working a long shifts as well as having to drive the distance on the horrible roads that it was getting her down. In asking other staff where they came from, she never found anyone who came as far to work as she did and quite a few of them were shocked. It was coming up to December and it was dark both ways and dangerous, and when Jacki moans about the road you need to take notice.

I am not sure if it was a problem with the roads or if that was just an excuse but the clear fact was that Jacki couldn't stay at the hospital for any length of time.

Perhaps Jacki went too soon but she got a job four days a week with a local pharmacist and took that instead, although the truth was; yes it was local but also far below her. She did have some good fellow employees there but actually there were some terrible ones as well and Jacki very soon realised she had made a mistake going there. Although the Pharmacist thought she was excellent we knew she would be leaving shortly. She had gone there because a local job became available but didn't really consider its long term use to her.

She had contacted the local nursing home asking if there was any work and been telephoned to say there wasn't but she would keep her in mind and was sure there would be some work available shortly. At the same time as this, she had to go the local job centre to explain our situation to them and they wanted to know why she was looking for a long term job. They felt she would be far better only working one long or two normal days a week and then topping up her income by claiming Carers Allowance. This seemed a fantastic idea to claim Carers Allowance and then to find a part-time job to top up her salary.

As had been predicted, the nursing home rang up and called her for an interview soon after this, to which Jacki went and she was delighted when they offered a job one long day or night a week. The nice thing about this was Jacki could be fairly flexible when she worked and, if I had a long journey because of some treatment, she could work around that. Jacki has been doing this for two years now and, whilst it is not the career she would have chosen when she went into nursing, it is an interesting job and the sad reality is that it is more important than a career move at this time.

Christmas came and it was a strange affair in that Jacki's mother came up but stayed with her brother and his wife and the only day we really saw her was Christmas day when we had lunch together at a local hotel. The Tontine was chosen as the restaurant by Jacki's uncle, who we were all happy with but they wanted us to start eating at three o'clock, which was terribly late for me but never mind. It was great that my mother-in-law came up at Christmas but we didn't really get a chance to speak to her at the hotel. Jacki's grandmother was brought with them, but unfortunately she is now very old and has dementia so it was lovely seeing her but, in reality, she wasn't properly there.

Shortly into the New Year I received a letter from the Driver and Vehicle Licensing Agency which told me they had now considered what had happened to me. They were quite happy if I decided to drive again but they also said I should look into having a lesson to remind me of what driving was about and also to enable me to regain some confidence.

Having my licence back meant a lot to me, because now I can drive if I want to, however, I drive only when I have to now. Most things in Peebles are a local affair for me and, whilst it might take some time to get there and several stops, I would normally prefer to hobble along to them. Anything that is further away, Jacki will drive. In the past it would probably have been Jacki who drove but now it is always Jacki driving. There are very few benefits of being disabled but they include the Blue Badge for parking and disabled bus card for going greater distances. So, with these resources behind me I don't need to drive much but at least I know I can if the need arises.

Although I don't do much driving, I thought I should follow the advice of the Driver and Vehicle Licensing Agency as well as my doctor and Occupational Therapist and have an informal driving test. One of the medical centres I go to in Edinburgh is the NHS Astley Ainsley Hospital and they have a specialist driving centre. I applied for a lesson with them. When it arrived, I was slightly surprised by how much was involved and they said I should allow two hours for it. Time was not often a problem and I allowed a day.

It started with me performing a series of tests run by a Physiotherapist to determine how serious my original injury was, including a test inside what had been created like a car and I had to pretend to be driving. This was far harder than any driving I had done before, or since. Apart from a situation where I lost control of the signals I actually managed to pass although my response times were a bit down on the norm.

A doctor came in briefly for the second section and she again asked questions of me and the crash. There was one point where my use of the English language let me down, and she took a very extreme view of what I said, even though there was no problem, when she told me, it sounded severe. We did manage to get over this problem when I indicated what I had said and what I meant. Unfortunately, because of the length of the day I have been unable to remember exactly what was said since, but I did get a clean report.

The final session was just over an hour and this was why I went. It was sort of a test and sort of a lesson but I drove around Edinburgh with the Physiotherapist just making sure I was alright. It was extremely hard work, but it was very good as I had a chance to test myself in a relatively safe environment before getting back to the centre and hearing what they had to say. Hearing their comments, it all made sense and when Jacki and I came to changing the car, we would adhere to them. In particular, they said I get very tired very quickly and I wouldn't be able to drive much more than an hour or so. Although an hour would be sufficient, it makes you realise just how affected you are. They said I would be able to increase this by buying and hence, driving, an automatic car. I had never really thought of getting an automatic before but it made sense and next time around it would be an automatic.

I still had a flat in London and two other flats. The truth is that I couldn't manage them anymore. Every time something happened the agent would ring up and he would say something and I didn't know what he meant. I would sell them all this year even though London was a great property and had gone up in value. Hopefully, that would cover the loss on the other two. I still had tenants in London until July and the agent was convinced he would sell it before then as it was early March, although for tax reasons I decided the sale should be after the fifth of April.

In about two weeks I had an offer at the full asking price on London and he was prepared to wait till mid-July when the tenants would go. This was excellent news because I knew the two northern flats would not sell so easily and I would have to use a specialist agent who would take at least twenty thousand Pounds off the price but they would go immediately. I am a disabled man and more mentally than physically, hence the thought of renting those flats out is just too much for me, so I would let them go as soon as was possible.

These companies are a bit hard-faced about it but they do work well and the properties got disposed of as well. Each property was let and they decided they would take them let which, from my point of view was brilliant, as I didn't have empty properties and the legal affairs were all covered. The upshot of this was that, when all the properties had been disposed of, I still had a few quid remaining which, considering the loss on those two, was fantastic and a bit surprising. This just goes to show how much London prices had risen because buying all the properties through a property club with the top two officials sentenced to jail, I had paid well over the odds for the flats.

I had been going to the Chest Heart and Stroke Scotland charity for a few months and when I was told by my Occupational Therapist that I should try and seek some voluntary work I initially went to the local shop to see if I could help them. They seemed very keen for me to help them but I was fairly depressed by the nature of the work I could do there. When I came home I sat down with Jacki and thought what I could do. I knew I could work in a shop if I had to, but in reality it was not what I wanted to do. Jacki suggested I should ring the service organiser I had previously become involved with and see if she had any suggestions.

As a result, I decided to ring her and she was actually quite excited. As always, I take a few minutes to catch up with people, which is annoying because historically they were usually behind me but now since the stroke they are ahead of me. After a couple of minutes, I realised what she meant and she was excited because there was potentially room in their own Accounts Department at the Head Office. She agreed she would have some words with the accounts team and they would probably call me in. I decided I would rather wait for this than apply to the shop and at least I had some good news for the Occupational Therapist.

It is fair to say that the internal workings of Chest Heart and Stroke Scotland are a lot slower than anything I was used to, but eventually they called me in for an interview. I say interview, but they had already decided that anyone who'll work for them free of charge will be given a chance and it isn't often they get a qualified Chartered Accountant put his name forward. The interview was a nice chat with the top two of the accounts team and the manager of volunteers. Unfortunately, the second of the accounts team has since retired although her replacement is equally as good, but because of this I had several weeks of not officially having a boss, but that was not an issue for me.

The role at Chest, Heart and Stroke Scotland has changed since I have been there. I was originally approached to do certain things with the Accounts Department, although travelling to Edinburgh has proved more difficult than expected. I now only go into Edinburgh every other week and this has reduced the time I have available for more specialist accounts work. In addition to this, they have realised I am more than happy to talk about what has happened to me, at a young age. Probably the best by-product of the North Pole was the need I had to talk about it in public. At first, I was fairly nervous but I soon realised as long as I was sensible no one else would ever know, so it did not matter if I was one hundred percent right or not. Having grasped this, it made talking about the North Pole very easy, and then it made talking about anything very easy.

As a result, I am more than happy to go to their events as a victim of a stroke, although they don't get too many of them. I should have attended two for Chest Heart and Stroke Scotland but so far I have only attended one. Whilst I say that, I am more than happy attending. It is amazing how little I am able to do at the meetings. The one I attended, I was due to talk about my experience of a stroke for a maximum of five minutes. If I had been told to talk about me for five minutes before the stroke I would just have gone and done it. I certainly wouldn't have had to make notes and to rehearse it so thoroughly beforehand, but now I had to make notes. Not only was I worried about not saying things but, more importantly, about getting the words completely wrong so they understood the wrong things, or more likely didn't have a clue what I had meant.

Even with the notes it was very difficult to speak coherently for five minutes and, the fact is, those five minutes took it out of me for the entire day. I had already planned for Jacki to come and fetch me and I am very glad she did. The other speech was due to be aimed at a local legal firm who had decided we would be their charity of the year, but unfortunately on the day of the presentation, they rang us up and said that, due to a conflict of interest, they could not have us present at the moment. I am not really sure what the conflict was but I believe it has now been resolved and hopefully we can do it next year.

On the plus side of this, one of the Solicitors contacted me and said that he knew a man who had had a stroke when he was forty one. He was the CEO of a company which he immediately had to leave and he then became a caddie at his local golf club. This was several years ago and, since then; he has written a book about dealing with a wholescale career change and gone back to the company but more as a consultant. He gave me his details and the book and suggested I called him and arranged a meeting.

He came over to my house one afternoon and it was excellent. It was fantastic to have someone come over who is totally familiar with the setup and fully understood what I and, probably more importantly Jacki, was saying about the stroke. He said two things which will always stick with me. Firstly, he said "I often forget things and I mention it to other people and they say I forget things too". "I used to try and point out the difference but now I just move on". That really stuck with me because it is exactly the same with me. Forgetting things takes on a whole new meaning. There are several things which I do that I cannot do anywhere near as well as before and, if I say I cannot do it because of the stroke, it does not mean a minor omission once in a while, it is a permanent problem.

The second thing he said stuck with me for a different reason and that is, he gave me incredible optimism. He said that for the first two or three years after the stroke he did nothing. Since then, he has managed to move forward and get things sorted out but for two or three years he was struck down by the effects of the stroke and achieved nothing. It was great having him over because he knew and understood exactly what I felt. It was interesting that he had to leave after about an hour to drive home and he was worried about driving home after having two meetings in a day. We were his second meeting as he had been to an Edinburgh meeting beforehand.

With Chest, Heart and Stroke Scotland I have also become a more significant Volunteer and now I am appointed to the committee that identifies the needs and actions for the volunteers.

Although my ability to help with accounting matters is very reduced from what was thought, I am able to help with key tax matters as I am still a registered Chartered Accountant. They recently had a value added tax inspection which has gone relatively well, although the inspector had a few queries and I was able to suggest the things they should mention. This was, for me, a simple case of acting for a client but seeing how appreciative they were made me realise just what I have lost from a working viewpoint.

I have been getting to know all the various sectors of the NHS who are relevant to me and there are quite a few. My General Practitioner is so effective and he heads up all the others, at least he always has a constant supply of letters from other specialists on his computer. From my viewpoint, he is excellent because he is so committed to his patients. The thing I most remember about him is when the Disability Living Allowance was changing to Personal Independence Payment and he asked me in a consultation what the biggest problem was for me with life. I started to give him some medical opinion but of course he knew that. What he wanted were the general problems for me with life. I didn't need a second chance and I told him those things I could at that point remember. He stopped me before I had finished with "that will do". The reason I remember that was because it illustrated he is prepared to think of me beyond a patient and think of me as an individual.

Although the General Practitioner is officially the main doctor for me, I liaise with a few other doctors around the area and it looks like I will be with these for some time. I have a Neurologist whom I visit around every six months and probably because he is South African, Jacki gets on particularly well with him. He always appears glad to see me and he puts huge amounts of effort into my visits. The meetings only appear to be like good consultations but I am absolutely blown away when I leave and when I look at the time it is usually about an hour later.

He has been very useful to me in telling me what is a consequence of the stroke and what just happens and can be forgotten about. Since I had the stroke, a few things have been wrong with me and it is very helpful to have him say "I am afraid that is the stroke and will happen again and again" or to have him say that it is not connected to the stroke, although that is rare. An example of that is when I told him I feel a lot colder now and he simply agreed with me and he told me I had lost the use of my internal radiator and I would now be colder than normal. He then said "well at least you haven't lost it the other way and are normally far too hot".

Although going to see the Neurologist can be quite sole-destroying because he is honest and at times brutally so, it does always make me glad when I go to see him. It is not his fault I have had a stroke and I look to him for honesty about the bare essentials of what having a stroke is like. I had no warning of the stroke, it just happened and I knew nothing about it beforehand. Moreover, as Jacki reminds me, I was not prone to having a stroke at all. Now that I have had a stroke, I want some help in minimalising its impact. I am getting the help and at least now the stroke damage is pretty much fixed so the problems I have, I know will be problems forever. That seems sad to say and it is, but at least I know they are genuine problems that need to be resolved.

I noticed this the first time I saw the Neurologist. He always comes out to the waiting room to call you in and help you walk. I didn't think much about it but then Jacki said he comes out to see you, makes his way over to you and, in particular, finds out if you are in a wheelchair or not. I don't know of any other doctors that do this and I find him very helpful.

I have some other doctors who look after me as well including another Neurologist at NHS Astley Ainsley Hospital at the SMART Centre. He was particularly useful to me in that he is a specialist head doctor and he was able to categorically state that I had been mentally affected by the incident and, therefore, completed the form for me to make me exempt for council tax, a form which we have subsequently used repeatedly to prove the serious cognitive impairment. Unfortunately, the General Practitioner had found it difficult filling the form in as the truth was, he didn't know, without all of the executive-level tests I still had to have done.

I see no end of other medical people at the various centres and I find it amazing that they are there free of charge simply because I have had a stroke. The next group of people I have seen are all of some description at NHS Hay

Lodge Hospital. Originally, I met the Occupational Therapist several times to see just how out of it I was. I had hoped to get back to work quite quickly although that was always technically impossible. She knew from the beginning it was not possible but because I had signed up for some treatment she gave it to me. As such I have always had a great deal of respect for her.

When I went to get measured up for a wheelchair which the General Practitioner had put me forward for, Jacki and I were slightly worried because I can walk and do always insist on walking as much as possible. The Occupational Therapist though was totally understanding of our situation and she said that my getting a wheelchair was totally sensible, even if I only occasionally used it. She said there was no doubt I would only use it where necessary and, what it would do, would give us the choice of staying out or not because it would help when I was fatigued.

Still at NHS Hay Lodge Hospital, the Dietician, who I had to see a few times because I had lost so much weight when I was on pureed food. Unlike most people I cannot seem to put weight on as a matter of course, increasing my weight was going to be a gradual thing. I, of course, knew this and although I always told her this, I wasn't sure at first if she believed me. By the end she did, and when I finally got my weight up to where it was pre-stroke she discharged me. Being discharged by the Dietician was a strange emotion because I'd never been discharged before. People have stopped seeing me and I have not needed them again so not called them but no one had ever said "that's all, I'm discharging you".

Another medical person I see regularly is the Podiatrist. The first time I met her she looked me in the eye and said we are not meant to cut toe nails anymore. I deliberately did not say a word and she then said "but for a stroke victim of course I will make sure your nails are properly cut", but if someone else was there they could technically refuse to cut them. I don't get too involved in the politics of the situation but it seems that a Podiatrist should be able to cut toe nails. I have always liked her because of this.

Having a stroke and losing nearly every bit of strength in my right hand side makes it virtually impossible to touch my toes, let alone cut the nails. Jacki does cut my nails but and NHS job should not fall on her. She cuts them in-between appointments, but knowing there should always be someone available who is experienced at dealing with my feet is very comforting. My feet will probably experience a lot of trouble over time because they get so cold. It stands to reason that from time to time something will go wrong.

The last people I see are not at all to do with the stroke and, instead, to do with my jaws being fractured. It doesn't really matter why you see them only because they are to do with my jaws fracturing; it becomes more of a long term commitment. The Consultant Orthodontist deals with my braces and is making sure my bite goes back together as much as is possible. Whilst she is fantastic with my teeth, I do always laugh when I leave her consultation room and it is probably very unfair, but neither Jacki nor I can understand most of what she says!

The reason for this is she speaks incredibly fast and clearly in a Scottish accent. I normally understand most of what she says by watching her lips, which I'm able to do because I am her patient, so she has to look at me when she is actually working on me and if she isn't working on me it tends to be me that she speaks to. Unfortunately, Jacki hasn't got that privilege so she finds the meetings incredibly difficult. Although understanding her is difficult, there is no doubt she knows what to do with the braces.

At the last appointment, she pulled a surprise on me. I knew that I would have three or four appointments left of treatment after nearly three years, but at this meeting she announced I would have to have other fittings. She spent a bit longer than usual with the fittings and added hooks to certain teeth, with elastic bands between my top and bottom teeth. This is irritating, but at least I know it is for a limited time span and then it will be over whereas the stroke problems will still be there.

She is treating my mouth in alliance with a Maxillo Facial Consultant. We have only met him a few times at various Scottish hospitals. At first the situation was that the Consultant Orthodontist would get the teeth to a state where a jaw operation would then be required to straighten everything together. We had been going with this in mind for almost a year when he suddenly turned round and said the brace was doing very well and he thought no operation would be necessary! I expect I should have been ecstatic by this, but he caught me totally by surprise and I actually felt a bit offended, although, once it had sunk in properly, I was very pleased. The situation is now, they don't believe I will need the large scale jaw operation but are going to see about a less aggressive chin operation. I can't get too excited about this, I am not sure why, because any operation is a big issue. I suppose I want no operation at all but if they must do one then make it as least aggressive as possible.

The final medical person I needed to see as a result of my stroke was a local Urologist. I had been having fairly minor, but repeated, urinary problems. I would go to the toilet and pass urine perfectly normally but I would be aware that urine was left in my bladder. I would then have to go again to empty my bladder. I asked the General Practitioner about this and he didn't seem worried at all but felt I should speak to a specialist in this field.

So an appointment was made at NHS Borders General Hospital. Notification came through the post with a long piece of work for me to do before the visit. I was required to keep a three-day record of going to the toilet. This was not too bad, but I had to manually fill the results in and it made me realise how bad my writing is, particularly when I am tired, so I ended up with a page of scrawl which I gave to him at the appointment.

Firstly the man looked at me and told me I was too young to see him. He then sat down and got his notes out and said "oh, you've had a stroke." At this point he said "you've left it a long time before seeing me". I felt I was being told off a bit, but I also took great comfort from this. The fact is, he considers that virtually everyone who has a stroke will also have urinary problems. He asked for the questionnaire which I gave to him embarrassedly but he seemed quite all right with the scrawl.

The appointment was quite comforting as it appeared it was quite normal for a stroke victim to have urinary problems, although he did want to see me again after a cystoscopy, which I have now undergone, to see if a catheter given to me when I was first in hospital has damaged my tube. He was fairly sure this was not the case but wanted to be sure.

The medical side is now a permanent nature of my affairs and it seems I am seeing one of them every couple of weeks, but I have also managed to fit in some special events. The first of these was my father's eightieth birthday where I went down to Brighton to spend the day with him. We decided to stay in Beaconsfield a couple of days beforehand and catch up on the news from my old firm. Not surprisingly, the firm had moved on and while there were certain people who still knew and remembered me it was surprising how many new faces there were.

Jacki drove me down to Brighton on the Saturday and, because it is not that far from Beaconsfield, we were able to take a leisurely trip down in the morning and arrive comfortably for me to be taken to lunch. Jacki did not join me. The lunch was at the same place as we had had our second wedding for the British family, although they had a smaller room this time. Once the lunch was over, I am afraid I was totally beaten by the situation and I had to leave my parents and try to settle down. Coming from Scotland, albeit with a stop at Beaconsfield, it was a long journey and combining that with sitting with my entire family and trying to keep up just finished me. I went home very pleased that I had come down from Peebles but absolutely shattered and a bit disappointed about that.

We had to come to London on a separate occasion because we needed to know if we could sue NHS Wexham Park Hospital for their negligence. We were given the option of attending by telephone but we felt that this was a serious offence and we needed to understand it fully. As a result, we again came down a couple of days early to make sure I was as fit as I could be for the event. As we were down for a couple of days I contacted the Receptionist in the office to see if anyone could come to London to see me. Not surprisingly, very few could come on a week night but the Receptionist and a Partner came for a night out at a restaurant.

This was a funny night because I felt like I still belonged up to a point, but then again, it was obvious I had left. Since I was no longer there, the company had replaced me as a Partner in the office, which was of course expected but it made me realise that, to them, I was a resource and if I wasn't available they would get a new one. It was, however, great to see these two people again and just to catch up with the news, well at least as far as was possible.

The real reason we were in London was to meet with my team of Solicitors and medical experts to find whether we had a case or not. We are in no doubt about negligence but causation is a tougher thing to prove and the meeting really centred on that, well at least I thought so because, to be honest, it went off at a cracking pace and centred on the medical opinions and really all I did was sit there. Eventually, I felt I needed a break and asked for the meeting to break for a few minutes which they readily accepted; in fact one of the key people went for a toilet break. We went outside for about ten minutes to let me wake up a bit and then went back to the meeting.

We were a little shocked as the meeting had carried on without us and, even more shocking, it had reached a critical stage. I thought we still had at least an hour of discussion to go, which is why I asked for time out, but it appeared they only needed a few minutes. The Solicitor who was leading the meeting just said "well we know what to do now so the medical people can go". We sat down with the legal people and they said we should send a letter to NHS Wexham Park Hospital and then wait. This was their recommendation, so we agreed. The ordeal has been extremely stressful for both of us and, unfortunately, unsuccessful.

One aspect of Peebles which has been extremely useful was my joining the local Round Table and this is mainly because they do a couple of things a month and are normal people who know about my illness but are not bothered about it. For me, it is very important to occasionally be able to go somewhere with someone who is not really concerned about the illness. Jacki is brilliant at what she does but she is always aware of the illness and it is nice to get away from it occasionally.

One such occasion was the Round Table Christmas dinner at a local restaurant. Most of the Tablers had been fairly busy doing a collection in and around Peebles. Unfortunately, I had been unable to do this because I am afraid when I got tired I would not be able to just carry on I would need to stop and I am not sure where I would be so

I had to stand down from helping them. They did, however, arrive at my house one evening and I made sure I said hello.

At the dinner I ended up sitting near to a one of our members, a General Practitioner and his wife. It was an interesting dinner, although to start with I was left totally exhausted by the set up. I deliberately arrived early because I knew I had to go up a flight of stairs. I agreed to do this because it was apparently only once in the evening and I knew if I could get there ten minutes or so before everyone else, I would be more or less recovered by the time they arrived. I did this and we were in the waiting lounge above the restaurant and they called us down.

Going downstairs is probably harder than getting up them, but this would be it for the evening and then I would sit down for dinner, so again I would have time to recover. I got down the stairs eventually, only to be told by the restaurant's manager they had made a mistake and we would have to wait about twenty minutes, so could we go back upstairs. I was totally exhausted and the thought of going back upstairs repulsed me so instead of going back upstairs I stood in the shop between the restaurant and the stairs to upstairs. I stopped there and told the others they could go upstairs but I needed to stay there and they got a round of drinks brought into the shop. I don't think the restaurant manager was that impressed but he wanted our custom and put up with it.

We eventually got in for dinner and it was reasonably good, although it did make me think what I used to do near Christmas. In the past I would have had several Christmas lunches and probably a couple of dinners as well as part of my normal networking, but this and Christmas day was it for me now. I felt quite embarrassed by this. There were some crackers made available to us and it was decided that we would join up around the table to pull the crackers, which seemed a lovely idea but my lack of strength meant that the crackers I held with the General Practitioner and his wife remained un-pulled. We had to pull them separately at the end so I could use both hands to pull them. No one was bothered and the General Practitioner and his wife were very nice about it, but I felt stupid.

As is always the way, as the night went on the more tired I got, to the point where I just could not stay awake. As a result, the time came for me to leave long before anyone else but that is something I am used to. I hunted out the then-Chairman to thank him for the night and say my goodbyes. It is fair to say that the Chairman had had a few drinks that evening, but as I shook his hand he just grabbed it and said thank you to me for what I had done for Round Table since moving to Peebles. It seemed odd because I don't feel I have done much as I compare this to my other Table days when I was healthy. He also mentioned he couldn't wait for the Round Table trip to

Barcelona. This was a very nice end to the evening although people need to understand my feelings on hand shaking.

I said I shook his hand because that is the action I made, but unfortunately I cannot shake people's hands any more, instead I hold them and wait for them to let go. As he grabbed my hand I could do nothing, I could not escape if I tried, so I just waited for it to end. In reality, it was only a few seconds but it felt so much longer.

The Chairman had mentioned Barcelona which is where he had chosen for the annual weekend away. It wouldn't have bothered me in the past but now it was a very big affair for me. The previous year I had moved to Peebles too late and I was not up for it so just let the people go without getting involved, but this year I got invited and didn't know what to do. It was sort of an organised trip but also the lads were away themselves and, I am sure, didn't want to worry about me. In the invitation e-mail, the Chairman had said if anyone has any queries to call him so I decided I would call him and see what he thought about me going.

I called him and he immediately popped round for a quick chat. I said that, on the face of it, I would like to come but I didn't know how I would react in a foreign country and if there were pre-set tours I needed to be sure they were manageable. I was very impressed with him because, firstly he came round when I had called him, so if it was difficult for me to go he could have just said so over the phone and also Jacki was at home so he had two people to deal with. The other reason was actually far more impressive in that he actually appeared to want me to go rather than accepting I might. He was prepared to change the plan to make sure I came.

I felt I had done my bit and the Chairman's encouragement for me to go made me say yes and so I booked on a weekend in Barcelona and more importantly my first holiday since the car crash, albeit only for four days away. I left very early Friday morning and I knew the trip had been organised, at least in part for me, as one member who was also going came to my door to pick me up first. With me in the car, he went to the middle of a nearby street and picked up a further three people he was taking.

We got to Glasgow airport perfectly all right and then I had to go through the airport to the plane. I had usually gone from Gatwick or Heathrow and expected it to be like them, but the other place I went from quite regularly was Southampton and it was more like that. I kept pleading I was disabled and apparently it made no real difference to the staff, although when I had to walk through the scanner, they accepted I took longer and they immediately gave me my stick back.

Whilst we were on the flight there was a group who were obviously on a stag do a few rows in front of us and when the stewardesses were giving the safety notice they copied all the actions. The funniest part of this was when they were talking about the life jacket and the whistle and the men simultaneously went "toot toot"! I am afraid, after this, they got a bit tiresome and boring but, never mind, I would leave them once the airline landed.

Once in Barcelona I had to have my wits about me in order to work out what I could and, more importantly, couldn't do. I decided I would stay with them for my meals and the morning activities whilst being fairly subdued in the afternoons. This was my theory but I felt it wouldn't happen like that. The problem I have with stroke fatigue is I am either alright or completely exhausted and I was expecting to just suddenly realise I had gone too far.

After lunch on Friday near the hotel, they decided to go down to the beach and asked if I wanted to go with them, which obviously I did and, initially, I said I would. After a couple of steps, I realised it was a fair way there and, as I have learnt, more significantly a fair way back so I spoke to the Chairman and gently dropped out. I am glad I did because I went back to the hotel and fell asleep. I knew nothing about the afternoon as I was fast asleep until a loud knock on my door at about half past six from a member of our group who said the rest of the group are in the bar and we need to go and meet them for a quick drink before dinner.

I had slept the entire afternoon but, was very glad I had, as it meant I was awake for the evening meal which is the highlight of our days away. As a result of this, I decided to keep it up even if it meant I missed seeing more of Barcelona than I could have done. I have decided that any other trip I go on I will follow broadly the same model.

A couple of big sporting occasions were on the Saturday and the Chairman had announced that we could go and watch Barcelona play football or go and see formula one testing at the circuit just out of town. I wasn't too worried about formula one testing, but the football would have been an exciting trip. However, the number of people around me would be very difficult to bear, so disappointingly, I told him I would be doing neither. One other person had also declined both, although my intention was to sleep in the afternoon and his was to explore.

The Saturday started and the two of us who weren't going to the events had decided we would go with the footballers and take a leisurely and long-winded sightseeing tour up to the football ground before we would leave them and get a tour bus back to a more central point and, for me, that would do for the day. I would then sleep for a few hours before our evening meal, whereas he would go on.

The morning was excellent as we went from the beach to the cable cars and then got on a hop-on hop-off bus which went around the top of the city and the football ground before coming back down to the beach. This was superb for me because I didn't have to walk much, but still managed to see a reasonable amount of Barcelona albeit from a bus and only seeing places outside rather than going in them, which I would have done in the past. Having dropped them off at the football we carried on to a Gaudi building where my co-traveller knew there was a café and stopped there for something. This was a great building and the café was excellent. We didn't say much, which I think made the other chap feel a bit awkward, but I felt exhausted and I knew I needed to get back to the hotel quickly.

I went to the toilet in the café and realised that my jumper had got stuck in my trousers. I am not sure exactly when it had got tucked in there but it must have been about one and a half hours ago at the last pit stop. This may sound insignificant but it is actually quite an important issue because it happens fairly frequently and there is something that makes me unaware to what is a fairly important cosmetic issue. No one in Round Table mentioned it, and I have never mentioned it to them, but I think they must have noticed. I would expect Round Table to take the mick out of how I was dressed but they may have been too embarrassed to mention it as they know about my medical background.

The next day we went for a trip round Barcelona in the morning, a decision I was regretting as most of the trip was on foot, but then I was lucky although the others were a bit annoyed. Firstly we were going to go around the cathedral but because it was a Sunday this was closed except for people praying. Whilst it was a shame we couldn't tour the cathedral, it did mean I could wait for the bus and sit down a bit more. The second piece of luck was the fact that the bus got cancelled and we decided to go for lunch.

After lunch we had effectively split up into two groups which, again, gave me a bit of help as now no one knew where you were. I went back to the hotel with a few people but, whereas the others picked some things up and left, I put my head down and slept. I awoke after about two hours and thought I would contact the Chairman to find out where they were but to my surprise five of them were at the hotel across the road from our hotel so I went and sat with them. I was expecting a move fairly shortly from there, but they seemed to be settled in and listening to them, they had already contacted the Chairman to tell him they weren't moving for the day. I think they expected me to go and find the rest of the group, but stopping for dinner right outside the hotel was for me excellent.

The next day was the journey home and it was simply a case of doing everything gently. We went into town to do some shopping but, whereas the others were constantly looking at everything, I just meandered up the high street and whenever the opportunity arose I stopped for a cup of coffee. I didn't have children to buy for, only a wife and I knew what she wanted, so I would get that at the duty free at the airport. I just dawdled up and down the street before we got the bus to the airport. This was the big occasion for me as I had everything with me so it was heavy and going to the bus was a bit of a walk but I had prepared myself well and I made it reasonably alright although I was happy when we were on board.

That was my first break since I had had the accident but perhaps the biggest achievement. The next was the first time Jacki and I had been away since the accident and it took a bit of thought but we decided on a cruise. Neither of us had been great fans of cruises before the accident but now it seemed ideal because we were always near the home camp and we could decide how far to go each day.

We flew to Barcelona and then cruised around Spain and Portugal before heading to Southampton. This was fantastic for me as we had three stops during the cruise and I was able to head out at each stop, but we never went too far. I think Jacki was a bit disappointed we couldn't go further. In fact, I was, but at least we went ashore and enjoyed a sample of each place. We used to make sure we saw a lot of places but now I am happy just to have gone somewhere and if necessary we can go back another time. Perhaps the most interesting thing about this trip is the fact that my clothes were so much lighter than back in Scotland. It was September and back in Scotland I was definitely wearing a jumper and perhaps a thermal top as well, but here I went out in shorts and a T-shirt. Thinking about it, I cannot remember a time since the accident when I had been able to go out without a jumper or in shorts, so well over two years, but it was possible in Spain in September.

This again made us consider moving there, but unfortunately languages are difficult now so I think going may be a bit difficult. Learning Spanish probably would have been achievable before the stroke but now I have enough trouble remembering English words that I used to use every day let alone trying to remember Spanish words which, frankly, mean nothing to me.

The cruise was quite interesting, if not for the reasons we had considered. Jacki had booked a disabled cabin for us and it was incredible how much extra space we had although we did need it for my wheelchair, in particular a turning circle. On the cruise my wheelchair was needed an awful lot because of the roll of the ship. Whereas before, I didn't consider the ship rolling, now it proved a major problem and so Jacki, once again, had to push me around.

Still we have decided that cruising is the best way for us to travel in the future.

Since we have been in Peebles we have been trying to sort the house out and get it just as we want it. We will be there a long time; probably the rest of our lives so we need to get the house right, but it is difficult. We had thought it would just be a case of getting local tradesman in to do the necessary and then waive a few cheques at them and it would be done. It has not transpired that way, whether it is because I am not as good at this anymore, or due to the local tradesman being local tradesmen who don't have quite understand the requirements I need, I am not sure. The main areas for us are getting the kitchen, bathroom and en-suite right. We had a group of people who looked keen but he rang up in January and agreed to come around and that was the last we heard from him. Considering they want to charge us over twenty thousand Pounds I find that incredible and it would not have happened down south. Even if they couldn't do it then they would say something but here you just get silence.

We have done better in the garden and a fair amount of the restructuring has taken place in that we have put more of the garden to lawn and created a bit of a patio. We still need more work done on extending the fence and the same thing happened as previously, agreement to come around and see us but we heard nothing from him.

There is one improvement to the house which has had dramatic results and that is the sun room at the back of the house. We knew when we bought the house that the old sun room needed to come down, because it was rotten and unbelievably, only single glazed. We survived with it the first winter but the condensation was terrible and we never went in the sun room because it was so cold. Even in the summer it wasn't really warm so we knew we had to get it done. We again contacted lots of local individuals to give us a quote, and to be fair it was probably too big a job for them, but they never said this and so we got no quotes from them. We also approached two far more substantial firms and we ended up hiring one which was exceptional. They understood my situation but, above all, they kept us involved with the process. They were lucky in that there was no rain whilst they were building, but even so they kept to all their deadlines.

It has been built several months now and it is, without doubt, one of the most used areas of the house now. I can spend hours just sitting on the sofa we have put in there and watching the birds we get in the garden. We always watched the birds and fed them, but now we have a comfortable viewing area we have got a lot keener and provide a great deal more food. When I was very young I went on bird walks to watch the birds and now I am not allowed to work I spend hours sitting at home watching them.

15   What happens next?

I have now been a stroke victim for approaching three years. Two years is an important duration for a stroke victim; because before then the medical people always say you will get better for up to two years, thereafter you are more or less stuck with it. So, now I know that what is wrong with me will always be wrong with me. It's funny, when they used to say that after a few months or a year I really liked them because it gave me hope but now I think of them saying it and I hate them. I know it's wrong but they have taken away the sense of hope. Still, never mind, I am where I am now and at least that means I can now move forward. The stroke victims I have met who suffered the stroke before I did have confirmed that.

I now know what I can't do or, at least, can't do nearly as well as I used to and have made plans to deal with it. I have had a lot of medical help since the accident and they have been fantastic but the one area where I feel I have been left to my own devices is the practical side of how you deal with a stroke. I have mentioned this to Chest Heart and Stroke Scotland that I would have liked a quick questionnaire about how the stroke has affected me and what I can get done about it. For example, my body temperature is badly affected; therefore I now know to wear thermal gear. I did not know that my coldness was a direct result of the stroke. The charity agreed with the concept, but I think they are hoping I will start writing it.

Whilst this is not a questionnaire as such, it would highlight the practical issues I have found after having a stroke.

The first thing to consider each day is what you have to do that day. Usually, it is simple apart from the usual daily matters of getting dressed, which takes a lot of time and eating. The answer, regrettably, is nothing! Normally, I don't do anything which I would have considered an active event during the day, but when there is anything that is to be done, I need to consider it so carefully. Whatever it is I need to plan for it as carefully as possible. If it requires going somewhere new I need to ensure it is planned for, although usually asking Jacki if she can take me is enough.

Something new takes so much out of me, even if it only one thing for a few minutes, it will take up my whole day. I will make sure I have the correct clothes and any special equipment and medication needed, set aside for me the day before to avoid wasting precious time on planning this. Whilst there is always a risk of doing something you didn't know about if someone else is involved, you need to ensure that you have considered all possible likely events, because if you get it wrong the probability is you will get very stressed very quickly and this will make you tired - and I mean tired.

My speech is normally adequate for most situations but particularly when I get stressed I find it very difficult to speak and the early problems with speech come back. When I first had the stroke I knew what I wanted to say but didn't know the words to say it and, worse still, was when I thought I knew the words and said something else entirely. When I am fatigued or stressed out I do resort to the old words which are simply wrong. As I said earlier, the worst example of this is when I call Jacki by my ex-wife's name, but there are other examples that are harder to work out. These speech problems are particularly apparent if I am discussing things with a group of people.

Speaking to a group I am not able to pick up the individual signs from people. Before this would not have mattered, but somehow I need to see what someone is thinking so I can adjust the future few words. One of the key problems I have with all aspects of life, but it seems to show first when speaking, is that when I get fatigued the ability to focus on things becomes very difficult. People who I am speaking to receive muffled words and probably not the words I want them to hear.

This is even harder if I am speaking to a group of people as I lack the intuition to address them properly, it takes a great deal of thought. As I get more and more fatigued the thought of talking becomes increasingly difficult. If I know I will be with a group of people later in the day then I make sure that beforehand the day is easy so I can relax. This is applicable to social as well as business events. So, I know I will have problems once I get fatigued, but how long will I get before I am useless? I used to think pre-stroke I would have around fourteen to eighteen hours a day where I was properly awake and alert. Now, I am afraid the answer is only two to four hours when I am properly awake, although one area which I am proud of is my ability to move the hours between days, at least to some extent. If I had to, I could probably make seven or eight hours one day although the next day I would be useless.

This was one thing I learnt from the South African Neurologist. He said imagine at the beginning of every week you wake up and for that week you have around twenty hours when you are what I would call alert. You can spend them all on Monday but then you will find the rest of the week extremely difficult or you could spread them across the week, but remember you will only have about twenty. This is really the reason why everything has to be planned. Previously I would have let things take the shape they want to take because I could always adapt, but since the stroke I am afraid that is no longer possible.

One area I have had to come to terms with is my own affected body temperature. This first came to light because Jacki was always asking me why I was putting my slippers on every time I got up in the night. She kept telling me not to bother but I would say it is cold and put them on. Given it took me ages to put my slippers on I am not surprised she got so upset, but we now know there is nothing we can do about this. Unfortunately, the

Neurologist also subsequently emphasised that there was no way of fixing this for the future. Knowing that it was a problem did, however, make it a lot easier to deal with. We knew this was a long term situation and so we went shopping and bought lots of thermal vests and trousers and also made sure my sock collection now included thick woollen socks as well. Even in the middle of summer here I usually still have to wear the thick woollen socks.

I used to do a lot of walking before I had the stroke and clearly my walking is affected but at least I can walk to some extent. Before, I would just walk and give it quarter of an hour per mile to ensure I would get there comfortably on time, but now it is different. I will still walk, but the maximum distance is much lower and will be well under a mile and I will give myself an hour for the walk, because now I will have to stop every couple of hundred yards. Usually a stop with the walking stick to support me is sufficient, but there are times I have to sit down. I now know where every public seat is in Peebles! Before, I may know a few from walking past them so often but I wouldn't be able to mention them all and, particularly those inside shops and other services I may need. That is for walking somewhere I know, if I don't know the area then I am afraid I have to ask for help. It also assumes that the journey is flat as I am badly affected by going up and down steps, a hill or any uneven surface. We chose a bungalow to live in because steps are so difficult to manage.

When I know where I'm going, I have to look out for steps or inclines, as even four or five steps will cause me to have to recover with the stick before moving on. If I go from home to central Peebles there is one set of steps about half way, but it is only one set. As the steps are long and shallow and probably twelve in number I can walk them, but even those steps are incredibly difficult and tiring to climb up or down.

As well as the difficulty in walking, I now have the added confusion of having to know where toilets are as I end up needing to go far more often than I did pre-stroke. Again, I know where all the toilets are in Peebles. Using the toilet far more often than I did which is now, we think, a side effect of muscular problems brought on by the stroke, I also have the problem that once I go to the toilet after I have been and think it is done with, I have the urge for another go. The Urologist has given me medication for this, but I do not want to be on too many pills every day. I already take pills for leg pain.

I have a very good pair of shoes that I bought when I was doing well as a Partner, previously for important visits at Barnes Roffe LLP. I only got to wear them a couple of times before I had the stroke. When I got the role at Chest Heart and Stroke Scotland I thought that, for the first day of this role, I would wear the shoes. I managed to get a lift there but I had to walk home. It is not too far and I would have had to do a bit of walking in the office but I got home and I was exhausted. I took off the shoes and slept for a couple of hours. On waking, Jacki asked me how long I had had the shoes to which I said I've worn them three or four times. She was horrified and she showed me how I had started to wear down the right sole of this pair and others. To this day, I don't know how I have done this but the fact is I have and I now accept that my walking is nowhere near as good as it used to be.

The above affect me as they happen to some extent every day, as such I am good at hiding the effects and the recoveries from people but there are a few things that catch me out. The stroke burnt out almost a complete side of me. As such, I have very little right-sided strength. Normally, I deal with this as other people are not affected by my strength but there are a few occasions when they find out. Handshakes, as mentioned, are one of these occasions. I still believe this should be done as much as possible because it is a good greeting and shows that you will act professionally in everything, but it is difficult. I don't really shake anyone's hand any more I hold it for them to shake and just leave it there until they have had enough. It works alright, but a good handshake is important and now I am afraid I don't have one.

The lack of strength also makes cooking very difficult for me in that I am permanently in fear that I will drop the dish and I have had a couple of very nasty burns because of this. I am getting more aware and I haven't had a significant burn for a few months but the memory of what can happen still haunts me. There was one incident which still haunts me particularly badly and I have already mentioned this earlier. The meal was fish and chips. I served the fish first and this should have been relatively easy as it is simply one on one plate and one on the other, but for some reason I had to press very hard to get the second fish out and in so doing I managed to scald the tops of three fingers on my right hand which was painful but didn't matter too much. The problem with scalding my fingers is that it knocked my confidence away when it came to serving the chips. I ended up with the dish on the inside of my left elbow which of course it burnt thoroughly and in so doing I moved my left arm and it burnt the outside of my elbow as well.

I feel a bit embarrassed about saying I cook because normally I am reheating some frozen meal usually originally prepared by Jacki. The only real cooking I do is a couple of mince-based meals which I know off by heart and even those I couldn't say I follow a menu. I am afraid that now I don't have the energy to follow a menu and, unless it is a very simple meal to cook, I don't bother. To me cooking is now a chore I would rather not do.

Fortunately, Jacki understands I am cognitively impaired and now preparing anything vaguely new or complex will not happen from me. She has tried teaching me how to cook but she realises the dangers for me with cooking so if we have something which needs properly cooking she will do it. She leaves me to reheat things, but she cooks.

There was one very bad situation when she had some chicken pieces to be cooked from scratch and, I don't know how I did this, but I obviously had not cooked them anywhere near long enough and they were still raw. In the past, this wouldn't have happened but, more importantly, if it had I would have put the chicken back in the oven for another half an hour or so. Now things are different. I have in my mind a time and that is how long they have. Clearly, I got the time for the chicken pieces drastically wrong but that didn't matter they had this time so I was serving them.

I used to enjoy watching a film or a documentary on television because it would while away the time and provide me with entertainment or some useful knowledge but now, because I have had a stroke, I no longer have the patience to follow a program through to the end. This is a real shame and even things such as sport which I would previously watch as live sport, I am not interested enough to watch anymore. I will put the live sport on, but invariably click the television over whilst it is still going. I am afraid I haven't got the energy or the ability to concentrate to watch an entire sporting event any more.

When I speak to my friends and I say I'm cold, or I can't remember that, it is amazing how often they will respond saying they are cold as well or they have memory problems as well. This used to get me really annoyed because I would know that, even if they did have a problem, there is no way it is as bad as mine. Their problems would just be a case of missing a few key elements every now and then, whereas mine are an ongoing, much wider scale problem. Now, I accept that the real problem is they do not know and I cannot tell them how wide my problem is.

There was one occasion when we were at a community forum for the public of Peebles and Jacki asked the organiser if he had a seat for me as I had had a stroke and was feeling weak. I didn't know him at the time which made his answer appear worse and, whilst he did find a seat for me, his response of stating "oh yes, I had a cold last week" was met with disdain from us both. What probably made this even worse was that he saw nothing wrong with what he said and he was meant to be a prominent local figure! As I say, I expect I would have been like my friends in the past, as I had no way of knowing what the true extent of stroke consequences are, but now I know, I make very sure I never say a comment like this. When I was first under treatment, I would be given exercises by local people, the idea being doing the exercises would help you to do things for real in the future. This made perfect sense, but I could never find the energy to do the exercises. Eventually, I realised that doing meaningless activities was not my thing and, much as I tried to do them, I would not. In order to combat this I found the best way was to give myself active tasks that I would do. For example keeping my fingers active and ensuring my speech remains at an acceptable level are the main reasons I started writing this book.

One other area I have had problems with is putting weight back on. I lost a lot of weight when I was in hospital because I was only allowed pureed food due to broken jaws. Unfortunately, I have never been that good at putting weight on so for me to lose as much as I did in hospital presented me with a problem. When I came out of hospital my personal weight was around forty three kilograms which was far too low, admittedly a reasonable amount went on quickly just because I was eating normal food again, but putting on the last few kilograms was very difficult. When I was on the Dietician's list for about a year in Peebles, it was a case of enhancing my meals by adding a supplement to the food such as oil, butter or cheese. Doing this, I got back to the weight I was before the stroke occurred.

The other problem with this is, since the stroke, I have no longing for a particular type of food. Pre-stroke I would walk past a restaurant and want to go in it, now I am just not interested. There were lots of meals Jacki and I would cook or have when eating out and we would look forward to the meal but, now I am afraid it is just another task of the day. I do not know why this is, but I suspect that several of my taste buds have been burnt out because now my desire for food is far less than before.

Related to the food issue is an issue with smell. Whilst I can still smell things, I am afraid it is a lot less than before. Sometimes Jacki has a bunch of flowers and she says to me "smell them, they are gorgeous". I take a deep breath and try to smell them but I'm afraid, at best, I get a slight whiff of them but usually I get nothing.

One other problem I now have is I don't really know where my body is. This may sound weird but because I have been affected everywhere to some extent I no longer know exactly where my body ends and so I end up frequently knocking things over or bumping into walls. Related to this is the fact that I don't know how much or usually how little strength I have. I will attempt to put on a rucksack and fail because I just don't have the strength and other times I almost knock myself over because I misunderstand how much strength was needed and put in far too much.

I suspect there are other problems which I should have just dealt with as well but I am not totally sure which of these problems are caused by the stroke. It is possible the problems would have occurred anyway given the car crash but the important thing from my viewpoint is they have all adversely impacted on my life and on someone else's. For this reason, although these are practical and non-medical problems I do believe that if someone designed a quick questionnaire for stroke victims it would be very useful.

Since I have been up in Peebles, the local newspaper seems to have taken to me. A local reporter first met me a few months ago after they had put an article in their paper that anyone who has some local information or a local person with interesting news speaks to them. Jacki e-mailed him with news about me going to the North Pole and, subsequently having a stroke and he immediately responded, first by e-mail but then he rang pretty much straight away. Having rung, he made an appointment to come and see me as soon as he was able to.

When he came around, he was clearly interested in the trip but, more importantly for me, he was interested in how I had had the stroke and why we decided on Peebles as a place to stay. Perhaps even more interesting, was that he thought we were capable of staying in Peebles, which at least for us is a positive. Peebles was the first place I have moved to with Jacki where it is a reasonable assumption we will stay in the area if not the same house until we die.

So back to the question of what happens next. The short answer is quite simple, I now know all of my inabilities which are seriously affecting me and so I know what I can or can't do. Given that these are pretty much set in stone the answer is quite simply, I will do what I can and, at the moment, that is fairly limited and includes bird watching and generally staying around Peebles.

The longer answer is probably more interesting but is effectively the same as the short answer but includes a few more specifics. The bird-watching is very much part of the plan because I can sit down and take myself away from my problems for hours at a time and, more importantly, this can be done at home. I never used to think much about whether I was at home or not, but now it is a distinct advantage. If I get caught by any problems knowing that I can just go to bed until they are resolved is a very important.

Having said that, I do like to potter around near to home and so I will still pop into town or walk around Hay Lodge Park. One of the great things about Peebles, at least for me, is the size of the town. It is only so big and everything is nearby, so for me it is fantastic, as I can head off and firstly I know where everything is, particularly where seating is and, secondly, if I get hit by any stroke problems I just go home.

When asked about what other things I will do, there are more problems but again it is just a question of being aware of what can happen to me now. It is regrettable and unfortunate that I have had a stroke and that having a stroke means that I have problems from now until I die, but they should now be set and so it is just a question of deciding what I will do if one of the problems hits me.

I have effectively had a new life from the 28th April 2013 and, whilst it is far less attractive to me than the life I had before, it is my new life. All I can do now is accept the problems and disadvantages of the new life and make sure I live and enjoy the new life. Well at least I can walk, sort of.

Appendices

1. The scenery

2. My team

3. Ready to go

4. Cleaning the tent

5. Midnight

6. Me inside the tent

7. Cold

8. Packing to leave

Made in the USA
Charleston, SC